Extended Schools and Children's Centres

A Practical Guide

Also available:

Every Child Matters: A New Role for SENCOs
Rita Cheminais
978-1-84312-406-1
1-84312-406-8

Every Child Matters: A Practical Guide for Teachers
Rita Cheminais
978-1-84312-475-7
1-84312-463-7

Extended Schools and Children's Centres

A Practical Guide

RITA CHEMINAIS

Routledge
Taylor & Francis Group
LONDON AND NEW YORK

First published 2007 by Routledge
2 Park Square, Milton Park, Abingdon, Oxon OX14 4RN

Simultaneously published in the USA and Canada
by Routledge
270 Madison Ave, New York, NY 10016

Routledge is an imprint of the Taylor & Francis Group, an informa business

British Library Cataloguing in Publication Data
A catalogue record for this book is available from the British Library

Library of Congress Cataloging in Publication Data
A catalog record for this book has been requested

ISBN10: 1-84312-475-0
ISBN13: 978-1-84312-475-7

Typeset in Adobe Garamond by
RefineCatch Limited, Bungay, Suffolk
Printed and bound in Great Britain by
MPG Books Ltd, Bodmin

Contents

List of Figures and Tables

Figures

Tables

Acknowledgements

Thanks are due to colleagues around the country whom I have had the pleasure to meet while on my travels to a number of local authorities, who have identified the urgent need for a practical resource to equip and support leaders and managers of extended schools and children's centres in developing, establishing and operating high-quality extended services, including wrap-around care, appropriate for the twenty-first century.

Special thanks go to:

my mother for her patient forbearance during the writing of this book over countless numbers of weekends and holidays. I sincerely hope this will not be the last book of mine that she sees;

Philip Eastwood, who continues to encourage and inspire me to write and produce practical resources for busy practitioners working in schools and children's centres;

all the senior managers and staff I have had the pleasure to support and work with in schools and children's centres, who have helped me to identify what the key complexities and issues are of running such provisions, and in assisting me in finding possible solutions;

all those professionals I have met from government organisations, higher education institutions and educational publishing, who have valued and promoted my work;

Theresa Best and Tracey Alcock, my commissioning editors for their belief in my ideas, and for their continued enthusiasm, support and invaluable advice and guidance throughout the writing and compilation of this book;

last but not least, all the staff at Routledge who have helped me immensely throughout the production of this invaluable resource.

While every effort has been made to acknowledge sources throughout the book, such is the range of aspects covered that I may have unintentionally omitted to mention their origin. If so, I offer my apologies to all concerned.

Abbreviations

ASB	anti-social behaviour
ASCL	Association of School and College Leaders
AST	Advanced Skills Teacher
ATL	Association of Teachers and Lecturers
BEST	Behaviour Education Support Team
CAF	Common Assessment Framework
CP	Child Protection
CPD	Continuing Professional Development
CRB	Criminal Records Bureau
CYPP	Children and Young People Plan
DfEE	Department for Education and Employment
DfES	Department for Education and Skills
EAZ	Education Action Zone
ECM	*Every Child Matters*
EHS	Early Head Start
EIP	Education Improvement Partnership
EMA	ethnic minority achievement
ESRA	Extended School Remodelling Adviser
FE	Further Education
FSES	Full Service Extended School
FSM	free school meals
G&T	gifted and talented
GCSE	General Certificate of Secondary Education
GDP	Gross Domestic Product
GEP	Group Education Plan
HE	Higher Education
HLTA	higher level teaching assistant
HMI	Her Majesty's Inspector
ICT	Information and Communication Technology
IDeA	Improvement and Development Agency
IBP	Individual Behaviour Plan
IEP	Individual Education Plan
INCO	inclusion co-ordinator
ISBA	Incorporated Society of British Advertisers
LA	local authority
LAC	looked after children
LDD	Learning difficulties and disabilities
LSA	learning support assistant
LSC	Learning and Skills Council

NAHT	National Association of Headteachers
NASUWT	National Association of School Masters and Union of Women Teachers
NCSL	National College for School Leadership
NFER	National Foundation for Educational Research
NI	national insurance
NPQH	National Professional Qualification for Headteachers
NPQICL	National Professional Qualification for Integrated Centre Leadership
NRT	National Remodelling Team
NSF	National Service Framework
NUT	National Union of Teachers
OFSTED	Office for Standards in Education
OSHL	out-of-school-hours learning
PCSO	police community support officer
PCT	Primary Care Trust
PE	Physical Education
PESSCL	Physical Education, School Sport and Club Links
PMLD	profound and multiple learning difficulties
PPA	planning, preparation and assessment
PRU	Pupil Referral Unit
PSHE	Personal, Social and Health Education
PTA	Parent Teacher Association
QES	quality in extended schools
QiSS	quality in study support
RE	Religious Education
SEF	self evaluation form
SEN	special educational needs
SENCO	special educational needs co-ordinator
SLD	severe learning difficulties
SSG	School Standards Grant
SSLP	Sure Start Local Programme
SSP	Safer School Partnership
TA	teaching assistant
TDA	Training and Development Agency
TESSS	The Extended Schools Support Service
TV	television
UK	United Kingdom
USA	United States of America
VA	voluntary-aided
VAT	Value Added Tax
VC	voluntary-controlled
VCS	Voluntary Community Sector
YISP	Youth Inclusion and Support Panel
YOT	Youth Offending Team
YSQM	Youth Service Quality Mark

The Aim of this Book

The aim of this book is to enable leaders, managers, co-ordinators and all those working in extended schools and children's centres to know:

- what their role and expectations are in the light of the government's programme for change;
- how to implement and meet the *Every Child Matters* five well-being outcomes for children and young people;
- how to provide appropriate extended services and wrap-around care in response to the identified needs of children, parents, families and the local community;
- how to work collaboratively in partnership with other multi-agencies, and private, voluntary and community sector providers to procure and deliver high-quality services;
- how to quality assure and evaluate the impact of extended service provision and wrap-around care;
- how to self-review, monitor and evaluate the *Every Child Matters* five outcomes for children, aligned to national standards and OFSTED.

Who the book is for:

- all senior leaders and managers in extended schools and children's centres;
- extended school co-ordinators, childcare co-ordinators, teachers, Learning Mentors, governors with extended school links;
- voluntary and community sector organisations;
- Sure Start managers, LA officers responsible for supporting the development of extended schools and children's centres, extended school remodelling advisers ESRAs;
- senior managers in Primary Care Trusts and Children's Services;
- school improvement partners;
- senior lecturers in higher education providing training to leaders and managers of extended schools and children's centres;
- all other frontline staff and professionals from the Children's Workforce (education, health and social care) providing wrap-around care and extended services to schools and children's centres.

How the format is designed to be used

The book provides a resource that can be used:

- to act as a point of quick reference for leaders and managers of extended schools and children's centres, and multi-agency services;
- to inform more responsive, inclusive, accessible community and extended service provision in a variety of educational settings;
- to enable pages to be photocopied for developmental purposes, within the purchasing institution or service.

Introduction

The pace of educational change is rapid in the twenty-first century. *Every Child Matters* marks a significant commitment to the nurturing and education of the whole child through effective inter-agency and community support. The underpinning philosophy, operating within an inclusive context, has five outcomes for children and young people. These are central to the government's programme of change for effective joined-up children's services:

- **being healthy** – enjoying good physical and mental health and living a healthy lifestyle;
- **staying safe** – being protected from harm and neglect;
- **enjoying and achieving** – getting the most out of life and developing the skills for adulthood;
- **making a positive contribution** – being involved with the community and society and not engaging in anti-social or offending behaviour;
- **achieving economic well-being** – not being prevented by economic disadvantage from achieving their full potential in life.

Children, young people and families should be able to make informed decisions about the support that they need, in the knowledge that organisations will listen to them and respond to their needs. This support takes the form of high-quality universal services such as early years education and childcare provision, personalised learning in schools and a wide range of opportunities and support for young people. This includes effective, targeted and specialist services for children with disabilities, those in public care or those engaging in offending anti-social behaviour.

School leaders and heads of children's centres will need to develop skills that will help them manage extended provision in the context of 'dawn to dusk' wrap-around care and out-of-hours learning activities for children, young people and families.

The government wants to:

> use Sure Start Children's Centres to spread support so that more families can benefit, while continuing to make sure that those in difficult circumstances have the first call on our help.
>
> (DfES 2004c: 23)

Children's centres are a key part of the government's strategy for raising standards and integrating early years education, healthcare and family support.

The government's vision is that:

> By 2010, all children should have access to a variety of activities beyond the school day . . . and to a core offer of extended services. . . .
>
> (DfES 2005h: Foreword)

Extended schools and children's centres make significant contributions to meeting the *Every Child Matters* five outcomes, acting as service 'hubs' for the local community. The Primary National Strategy made clear that primary schools should be linked to their local communities, and that this might take the form of extended school provision. It goes on to comment:

> Extended schools support standards because they take a wider approach to supporting children's learning.
>
> (DfES 2003f: 51)

Extended schools are therefore seen to have a dual role: to help raise standards *and* support the wider community. This acknowledges the link between children's circumstances and their learning, but it does not necessarily mean that once a child's external barriers to learning and participation have been removed that their learning difficulties will disappear. They may not, especially if no changes are made in relation to tailoring teaching and providing appropriate personalised learning experiences.

Clearly, services for children and young people delivered in extended schools and children's centres need to become far more user-centred and solution-focused. They need to be able to deliver improved personalised outcomes through participation and ensure users are active participants in the shaping, development and delivery of education and related services.

Personalisation in this context means service providers and users being able to work together to create the services that best meet and respond to local needs. The greatest challenge by far for leaders and managers of extended school and children's centres is the management of the wide range of multi-agency partnerships.

Carol Campbell (2002) commented on inter-agency collaboration for inclusive schooling:

> In seeking to incorporate more services, collaborate with more agencies and extend school hours, there is a need to consider what is desirable and what is feasible. Included in such considerations are questions about funding and sustainability.
>
> (Campbell and Whitty 2002: 109–10)

New role for extended school leaders and heads of children's centres

Regenerating and transforming local communities through children's centres and extended school provision will require school leaders and heads of centre to be:

- **able to engage with the local community, maximising upon its richness and diversity;**
- **'solution assemblers', developing and building capacity in other staff;**
- **advocates for children young people, parents/carers and families;**
- **'commissioning agents', brokering and mobilising resources and services;**
- **'change champions', encouraging others to take a wider community view;**
- **'quality assurers' for children's centre and/or extended school provision;**
- **networkers seeking productive partnerships with a range of stakeholders;**
- **strategists for inclusion policy and planning;**
- **innovators and risk-takers seeking new opportunities to secure sustainability;**
- **facilitators of coherent and collaborative multi-agency team working.**

While school leaders and heads of children's centres generally accept the direction of the Children's Services agenda, they have concerns about 'the how'. Work–life balance for school leaders is becoming a major concern. Seventy-one per cent of headteachers are working longer hours because of changes to reduce teachers' workload, according to a 2006 Headspace survey. The same survey identified 27 per cent of headteachers are prepared to quit if their workload is not reduced.

The extended school initiative, as part of *Every Child Matters* strategy, clearly brings an increased workload. One possible solution may be to consider blended co-leadership of extended schools. This would entail one partner leader having a health, social services or business management background and the other having an educational background. Shared responsibility is the way forward in the effective management of this huge change agenda.

The Government White Paper (2005), identified the need to:

> . . . ensure that different services working with the same child do so coherently.
>
> (DfES 2005l: 74)

Every school matters and every children's centre matters because they each play an important and fundamental part in holding communities together and in achieving the five *Every Child Matters* outcomes. They do this through the provision of universal services.

The DfES considers that:

> An extended school is a school that recognises that it cannot work alone in helping children and young people to achieve their potential, and therefore decides to work in partnership with other agencies that have an interest in outcomes for children and young people, and with the local community. In doing so, it aims to help meet not only the school's objectives but also to share in helping to meet the wider needs of children, young people, families and their community.
>
> (Piper 2005: 2)

This book complements the ContinYou/DfES series of practical 'know how' guidance leaflets, which focus on specific aspects of operating extended school provision, and the Sure Start Children's Centres Practice Guidance, issued in 2006.

It provides a comprehensive overview of how school leaders, extended school co-ordinators, and heads of children's centres can meet the requirements of the government's change for children programme.

While this book alone cannot hope to resolve all the concerns and issues raised by school leaders and heads of children's centres, it does give signposts to further sources of information, checklists, practical guidance and pointers for further discussion.

The government's change for children programme is best viewed as being evolutionary rather than revolutionary. A ten-year programme of development and incremental change, it poses an enormous challenge to school leaders. This book is intended to help school leaders meet that challenge.

1

The Development of Extended Schools and Children's Centres

EXTENDED SCHOOL

The origin of extended schools

The extended school is not a new concept. Schools have been providing additional services and extra-curricular activities for many years. The forerunner of the extended school was the community school, dating back to the 1920s, when village colleges were introduced in Cambridgeshire. These enabled rural communities to provide a range of additional services for children and adults. Community schools began to develop throughout the country, largely in areas of social deprivation, during the 1970s and 1980s. The study support (out-of-school-hours learning (OSHL)) programme was another significant precursor of the extended school initiative. This was first developed in 1997 by the DfEE and The Prince's Trust. Schools in Education Action Zones (EAZ) and those serving disadvantaged communities were targeted for the programme. This was a good example of school partnerships working with other local providers and charitable organisations, such as Education Extra (now ContinYou), Business in the Community, Kids Club Network (now 4Children), to provide a wide range of activities. These included: breakfast clubs, homework and study support clubs, sports, music and other creative arts, interest clubs in ICT and languages, learning about learning (study and thinking skills). Learner-centred study support was a voluntary activity undertaken by children and young people, aimed at raising motivation, self-esteem, achievement, attitudes and attendance.

DfES research into study support undertaken in 2004 found that:

> extensive involvement of young people in study support activities gave them the opportunities to develop skills of participation, to take leadership responsibilities and develop peer support expertise, which could lead to self-regulated learning, social inclusion, improved social skills and respect for others in mainstream classroom settings.
>
> (DfES 2004a: 1)

Study support is central to the government's key strategies of *Every Child Matters* (ECM) and personalised learning, as it enables children and young people to fulfil their potential.

Australia and the USA have had extended full-service schools for the last 20 years. The USA models of extended school delivery vary from fully integrated and re-conceptualised education systems for social and health service delivery, to smaller-scale additions or extensions to the traditional individual school. They adopted an inclusive holistic approach to providing support for learning and well-being, unlike England emphasising attainment. Extended schools in the UK, as a development of the community school and study support programme, vary according to community need, geographical location and the amount of different funding sources available. There is no blueprint for extended service delivery, or for what an extended school should look like, as they operate in a permanent state of flux. Extended schools are undoubtedly an improvement on the existing nineteenth and twentieth-century school provision. This is because they are able to shape their extended services more appropriately, to address the out-of-school difficulties of more vulnerable children, young people and their families, resulting from the social pressures and changing demographics of the twenty-first century. The stresses of contemporary living, resulting from parental divorce, poverty, health problems, domestic violence or child abuse, can often lead to the associated out-of-school difficulties (the 'new morbidities') like depression, suicide, drug and alcohol misuse, in vulnerable children and young people.

> Full service schools are indeed the wave of the future. They are responsive to today's problems. They are potentially cost-effective and they are well received by students, parents and school people.
>
> (Dryfoos 1994, quoted in Calfee *et al.* 1998: 131)

Baroness Catherine Ashton also acknowledged the extended schools' valuable role in addressing children's problems:

> Having key professionals such as health workers, psychologists and youth workers based on school sites and working closely alongside teachers means that children's problems can be addressed more effectively, with less disruption to their learning.
>
> (DfES 2002b: 4)

There is a realisation that schools alone cannot solve these out-of-school problems, associated with multiple disadvantage and social exclusion, that create barriers to learning and participation. Extended schools fully acknowledge that multi-agency services, operating from within or near the site of a school, can help to address and improve pupils' poor school attendance, their poor attitudes to education and their underachievement.

The concept of extended schools

The government defines an extended school as being:

> One that provides a range of services and activities often beyond the school day to help meet the needs of its pupils, their families and the wider community.
>
> (DfES 2002b: 5)

A full service extended school provides a more comprehensive range of co-located services on a single site, provided by non-educational agencies such as health and social care, including adult learning and community activities, study support, and 8a.m. to 6p.m. wrap-around childcare. Both types of extended schools act as community 'hubs', providing a one-stop service.

Every school will not be expected to provide or manage the entire core offer of services themselves. Schools may choose to develop extended provision across a cluster of schools, each delivering aspects of extended services and activities, or commission existing local, private or voluntary sector providers, in order to ensure that the 'core offer' for their phase of education is available across the cluster.

John Craig (2004) identified the aim and purpose of extended schools for pupils:

> Extended schools enable pupils to learn in different places and contexts, helping them to pursue their own interests, make choices and escape situations that are counter-productive. They create spaces in which young people can relate to adults in new ways, that go beyond the formal, unequal and confrontational.
>
> (J. Craig *et al.* 2004: 55)

The underpinning philosophy of extended schools is the promotion of social well-being, i.e. taking a holistic approach to meeting the needs of local populations, in order to improve educational achievement.

The government has a clear vision of how children's trusts, children's centres, extended schooling and *Every Child Matters* dovetail together. School leaders are struggling with how to put the government's vision of extended schooling into practice.

Extended schools are more than educators of children and young people, as illustrated by figure 1.2. Their fundamental task is to maximise attainment through a family and community context that is supportive of learning.

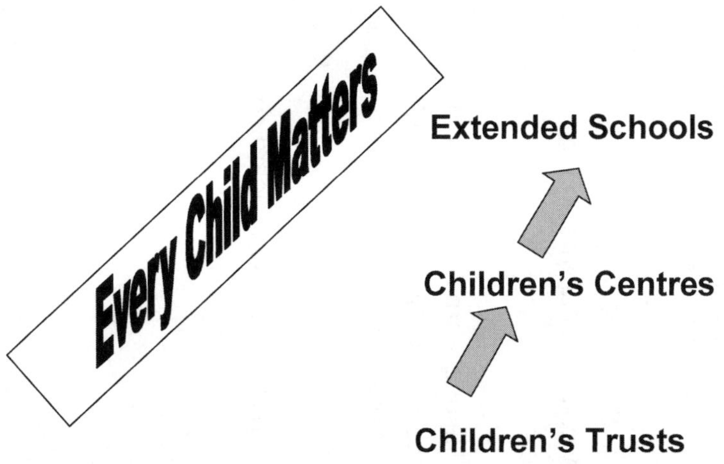

Figure 1.1 Government's vision for dovetailing universal service provision

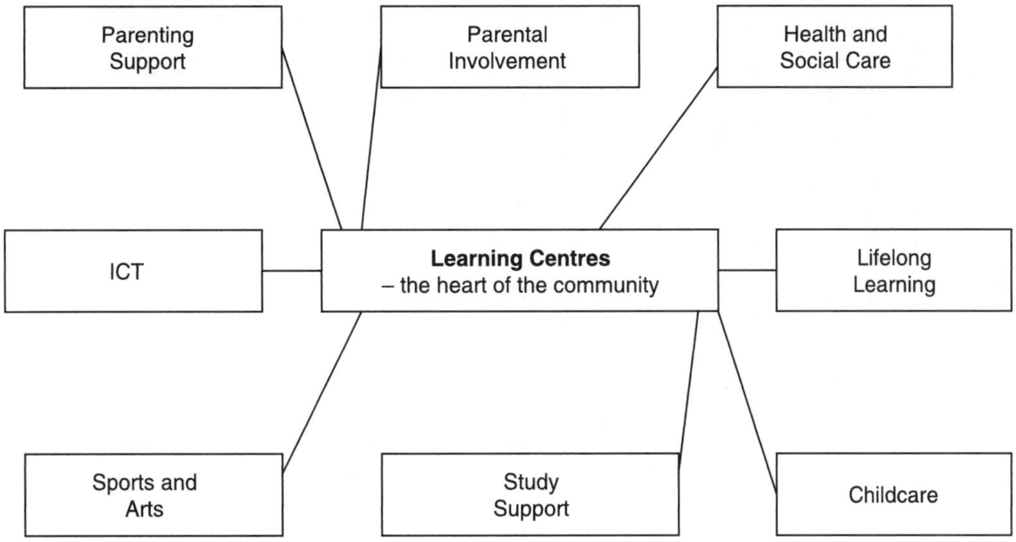

Figure 1.2 Extended school provision for the whole community

Extended schools core offer

The government wants to see the core offer in, or accessible through, all extended schools by 2010. The core offer comprises of:

- **high-quality wrap-around childcare** provided on the school site or through other local providers, with supervised transfer arrangements, where appropriate, available 8a.m. to 6p.m. all year round.
- **a varied menu of activities** being on offer, including homework clubs, 'catch up' and 'stretch' activities, study support, sport, music tuition, dance and drama, arts and crafts, special interest clubs such as chess and first aid courses, volunteering, business and enterprise activities, visits to museums and galleries, learning a foreign language.
- **parenting support** including information sessions for parents at phase transfer, information about national and local sources of advice, guidance and information, parenting programmes run with the support of other children's services and family learning sessions to allow children to learn with their parents.
- **swift and easy referral** to a wide range of specialist support services such as speech therapy, child and adolescent mental health services, family support services, intensive behaviour

Table 1.1 The Maple School Extended School Programme

WELCOME TO THE MAPLE EXTENDED SCHOOL PROGRAMME

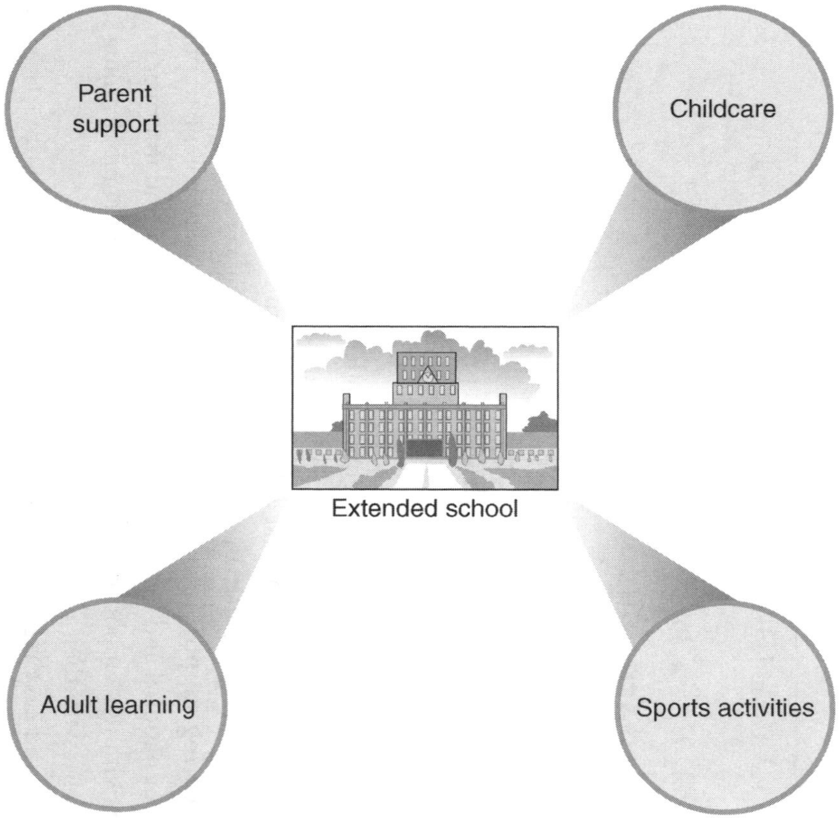

- Maple School, as a fully inclusive extended school, provides a range of services and activities, beyond the school day, to meet the needs of the whole child, families and the community.
- The extended school provision at Maple School is unique, as it is tailored to meet needs, as identified by children, parents and the community.
- The leisure and recreational activities, lifelong learning opportunities and the personalised services on offer to pupils, their families and the community promote a real sense of belonging, achievement and well-being for all.
- *Every child matters*, and everyone matters in this school's learning community.

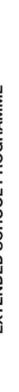

THE BENEFITS OF EXTENDED SCHOOL PROVISION

- Our extended school service provision is inclusive, accessible, flexible and appropriate.
- It takes place in an environment that is caring, safe, welcoming and vibrant.
- The use of ‘state of the art’ facilities and reputable service providers, ensures good-quality extended school provision is available.
- The extended school programme provides good value for money.
- Maple school extended school provision is held in high regard by the local community.

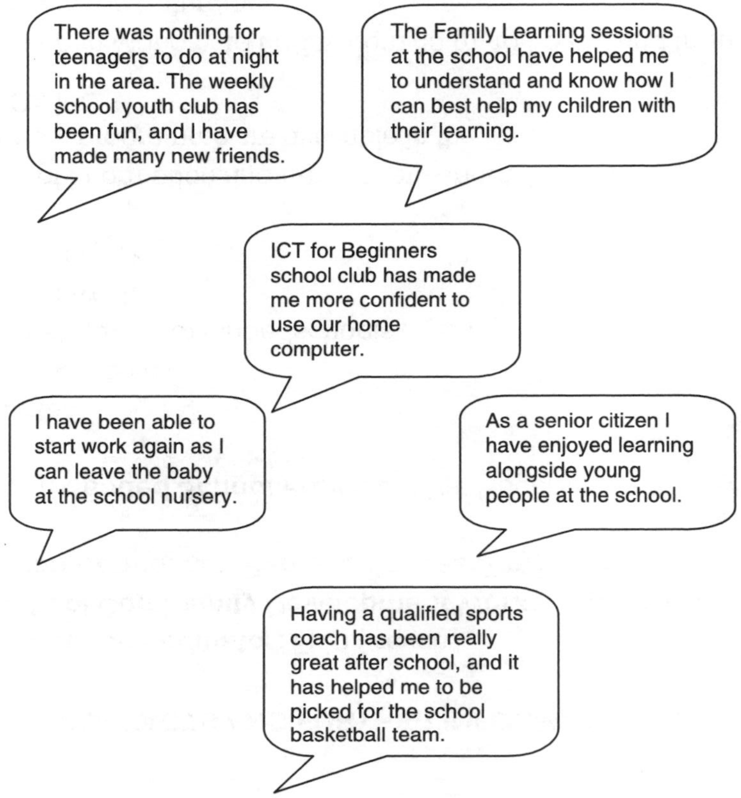

There was nothing for teenagers to do at night in the area. The weekly school youth club has been fun, and I have made many new friends.
The Family Learning sessions at the school have helped me to understand and know how I can best help my children with their learning.
ICT for Beginners school club has made me more confident to use our home computer.
I have been able to start work again as I can leave the baby at the school nursery.
As a senior citizen I have enjoyed learning alongside young people at the school.
Having a qualified sports coach has been really great after school, and it has helped me to be picked for the school basketball team.

Table 1.1 *(Continued)*

MAPLE SCHOOL PROGRAMME OF EXTENDED SERVICES	KEY CONTACTS AND FURTHER INFORMATION
Childcare provision: Nursery, Playgroup, Créche, Parent and Toddler group **Youth services**: Youth Club, Summer School and Easter Schools **Out-of-hours learning**: breakfast club, homework club, study support, sports, music tuition, dance, drama, arts and crafts, special interest clubs, health and fitness club, learn a language club, visits to museums and galleries **Specialist services**: referral and access to speech and language therapy, family therapy, counselling service for young people **Support for parents**: Family Learning, Parent Workshops, Parent Information Centre, Family Room **Community use**: ICT, Sports and Arts facilities, Adult Learning, Cyber Cafe	**Extended School Co-ordinator:** Fran Stevens **Extended School Community Development Worker:** Joe Taylor **Parents' Action Community Representatives:** Tim Connor Jean Trotter **Governor for Extended School Provision:** Pat Rogers **Useful Websites** www.mapleextsch.co.uk www.teachernet.gov.uk/extendedschools www.4children.org.uk www.continyou.org.uk A good range of information and free leaflets about the Maple extended school programme are available in the Parents Information Centre. This Centre is open Monday to Friday from 8a.m. to 6p.m., and from 10a.m. to 12 noon on Saturday.

support and (for young people) sexual health services. Some services may be delivered on school sites.
- **providing wider community access** to ICT, sports and arts facilities including adult learning.

The core offer ensures that all children and parents have access to at least a minimum of services and activities within their community.

Extended schools delivery models

There are four models for the delivery of extended school provision. The model(s) selected will depend on the school's resources and objectives. A school is likely, however, to utilise more than one delivery model. The four models of delivery are as follows:

- direct delivery – schools (governing bodies) make arrangements themselves, employing staff, and administering;
- delivery with third parties – working in partnership with existing local, private or voluntary sector providers;
- linking with other schools as a cluster, Education Improvement Partnership (EIP), federation;
- co-locating with a children's centre.

Four philosophical approaches to extended school service delivery

Extended school provision can be based on its philosophy of engagement with the community, and not just by its range of provision. Four different approaches are represented by the following table.

Table 1.2 Four philosophical approaches to extended school service delivery

Life Skills Centre (Social Capital) Voluntarism and trust Therapeutic activity Family Learning	**Knowledge Exchange** (Intellectual Capital) Exchanges of information Experimentation and Enquiry Training
Multi-agency Service Centre (Organisational Capital) Holistic local approach Co-location SEN provision and inclusion	**Regeneration Hub** (Human Capital) Co-production Job and enterprise creation Workplace learning

Extended schools, on this basis, need to invest in particular forms of capital (immaterial assets), which can help to focus and frame consultation with staff, parents, community members and pupils about the nature of extended activities and services required by users.

Personalised services in extended schools

The *Every Child Matters* agenda acknowledges the need for a personalised offer of extended services, which takes account of the variations in the needs of an individual child at different times. The *Every Child Matters* five outcomes for children offers a deep moral basis to personalisation, in that they give credence (status and significance) to a focus on the well-being of every child, securing entitlement to success and achievement.

Wrap-around services based in and around the school site are personalised (customised and tailored), in order to avoid the 'one size fits all' uniformity, thus enabling schools to educate children more effectively. The term wrap-around refers to extended school provision that is literally 'wrapped around' the normal school day, e.g. childcare, health and therapy services. Core assertions about the nature of personalised services in extended schools can be summarised as follows:

- services are designed in response to the defined needs of users (children, young people, their parents and families);
- users are partners in the design and development of future provision;
- users are able to make valid self-directed choices about service provision;
- providers of personalised services are accountable to their users.

Extended school development principles

Six underlying principles essential to the development of the extended school are as follows:

- shared leadership;
- inclusive culture;
- proactive change team;
- broad collaboration;
- proven process;
- rational political and emotional considerations.

These six principles all help to break down barriers, maximise capability and increase capacity within the developing extended school. An example where these six principles were utilised was in the development of a co-located secondary PMLD/SLD special and mainstream school, on one site. Two contrasting school cultures and organisations were brought successfully together through strong co-leadership and a team approach, to incorporate integrated multi-agency services and wrap-around care for the entire campus.

Factors influencing the development of extended schools

Table 1.3 Factors influencing the development of an extended school

Facilitating factors	Inhibiting factors
■ Vision of the school leader ■ Access to resources ■ Commitment and joint working ■ Appropriate level of resourcing and management ■ Effective discussion and communication with partner agencies regarding protocols, roles and collaborative partnership working ■ A model grounded in the contexts and needs of the particular community	■ Lack of space ■ Lack of sustainable resources ■ Low levels of community interest and involvement ■ Top-down imposition

The government's expectations for extended schools

By 2006 there will be at least one full-service extended school located in an area of social disadvantage, in each local authority.

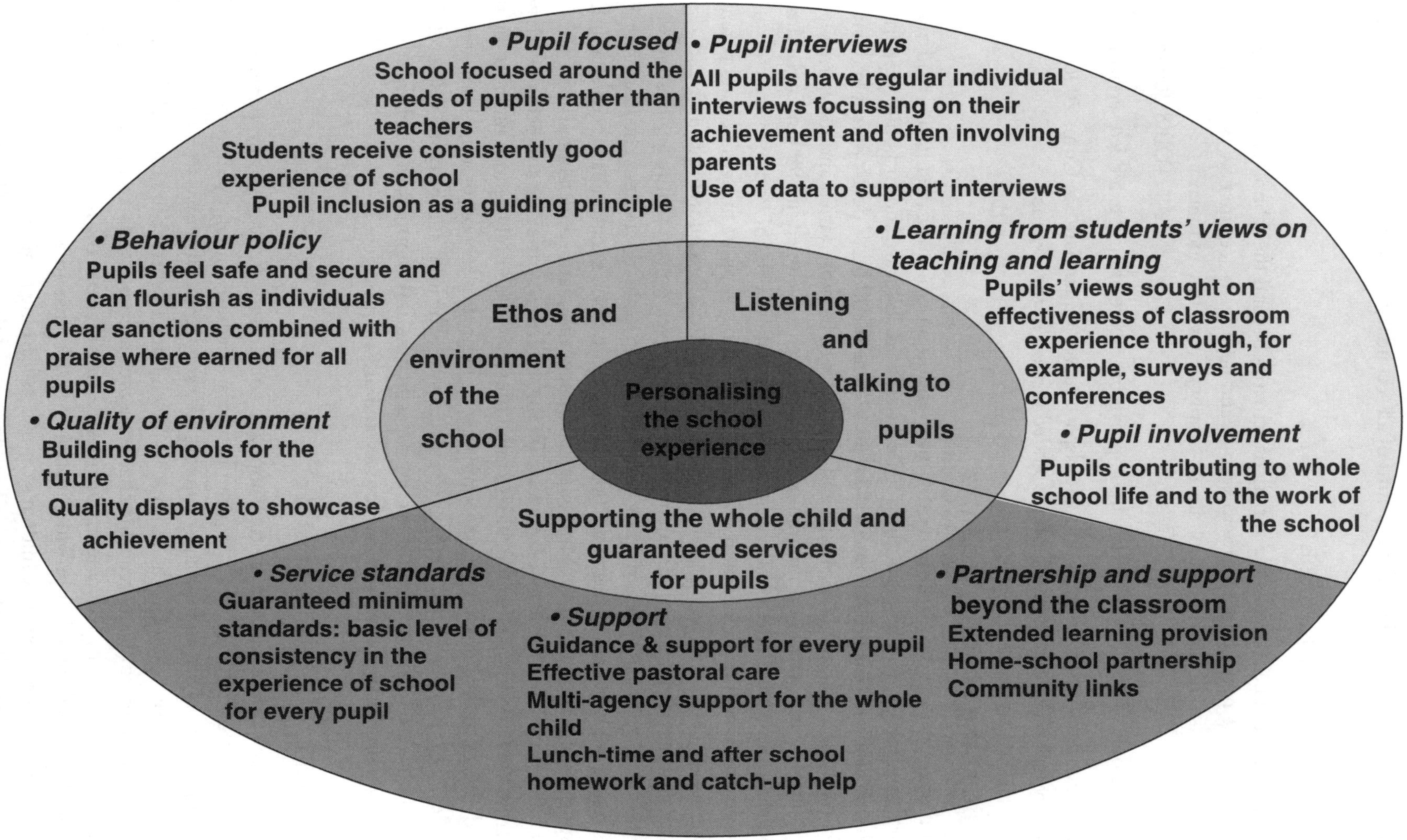

Figure 1.3 Personalising the extended school experience: school organisation and beyond the classroom. Source: G. Last (2004) *Personalising Learning: Adding Value to the Learning Journey through the Primary School.* London: Department for Education and Skills.

By September 2006, 2,500 schools (10 per cent) will have extended hours, opening from 8a.m. to 6p.m., providing access to the core offer of services.

By 2008, half of all primary schools and a third of all secondary schools will provide a core offer of extended services.

The government's pledge is that by 2010

> 'all children should have access to a variety of activities beyond the school day' and that these will give them 'the opportunity to keep fit and healthy, to acquire new skills, to build on what they learn during the school day or simply to have fun and relax'
>
> (DfES 2005h: 4)

By 2010, all schools will be an extended school, providing a core offer of extended services.

Thirty-seven per cent of headteachers' in a Headspace survey (Guardian/Ed. Coms 2006), indicated they had no intention of offering extended services at their school.

The origin of the children's centre

The USA pioneered a narrowly delivered early-intervention programme called Early Head Start (EHS) for disadvantaged families, that provided centre-based childcare and/or family support through home visiting. This programme was found to benefit children's development and family functioning. England took the USA model and adapted it to be more varied and less narrowly focused. Thus, the Sure Start Local Programmes (SSLPs) were developed in 1999 in England, and were designed to support children under four and their families. The SSLPs provided a core of integrated services which included: outreach and home visiting; support for families and parents; support for good-quality play, learning and childcare experiences for children; primary and community health care and advice about child health and development; family health support for people with special needs, as well as helping with access to specialised services. The first phase of children's centre implementation began in 2004–06. Many children's centres have been established from existing settings such as SSLPs, Mini Sure Starts, new and planned Neighbourhood Nurseries (2001) and Early Excellence Centres (2003). Children's centres are also being developed from other existing provision, which includes school nurseries and family centres provided by the maintained, private and voluntary sectors. Some may be located in schools or, on school sites, operating flexibly to be open in the evenings or at weekends. The local authority has responsibility for the development of children's centres, acting as facilitators and commissioners of services through the Children's Trusts and other voluntary and private providers.

The concept of children's centres

Sure Start children's centres act as one-stop shops and community service hubs for parents and children under five, offering early education and childcare ('educare'), family support, health services, employment advice and specialist support on a single site, with easy access for parents and easy referral between services. The purpose of the children's centre is to reduce child poverty and social exclusion, improve children's life chances as well as improve outcomes for young children from birth to five, by reducing inequalities existing between the most disadvantaged children and those less deprived. It provides inclusive services that are responsive to local community needs and preferences. Children's centres, as learning communities, aim to develop service users' self-esteem, self-confidence, self-fulfilment, and their 'voice'. They help to promote lifelong learning, help parents and families have more control over their lives and manage change.

Provision in children's centres

There are three broad levels of service provision available at children's centres, based on the level of needs of families and children under five in the local community.

Table 1.4 Levels of service provision in children's centres

Level 1 – Universal provision for all families and children under five
▪ Free integrated early years education and care for 12.5 hours a week, 33 weeks a year for 3 and 4 year olds, increasing to 38 weeks a year from 2006, and eventually to 48 weeks ▪ Information and access to childcare in the local area ▪ Information on parenting, drop-in groups and opportunities to access parenting support and education ▪ Ante-natal and post-natal services and child health services and information on health ▪ Information about employment, education and training ▪ Information at transition points, i.e. at birth of the child, entry to primary school
Level 2 – Provision for families experiencing challenging circumstances, leading to their children being at greater risk of obtaining poor outcomes
▪ Advice and support in accessing care for under-threes ▪ Group-based ante-natal and post-natal support focused on parenting ▪ Varying levels of group-based or one-to-one parenting and family support to meet the distinct needs of fathers and mothers ▪ Employment and training support
Level 3 – Specialist support and provision for children identified as being at an even greater risk of poor outcomes
▪ Intensive structured parenting, child and family support through evidence-based programmes including outreach and home visiting. This includes practical day-to-day support in the home, delivered together with other agencies like social services. ▪ Access to specialist services such as speech and language therapy, family therapy, safeguarding services for children who are at risk of harm, abuse, neglect.

Delivery models for children's centre provision

The delivery model for provision in children's centres varies according to the level of needs in the local area. In the poorest most deprived areas a full-service delivery model will operate that brings together children's services and childcare. In the less disadvantaged areas a lighter touch delivery model operates, which focuses on the provision of information and co-ordination.

Children's centres and multi-agency working

Delivering children's centre services requires a range of agencies and organisations to work together. Local authorities working with Primary Care Trusts (PCTs) through Children's Trust arrangements are able to develop effective multi-agency arrangements for children's centres. Multi-agency services are normally co-located in the children's centres in the most disadvantaged areas. A multi-agency approach requires a common vision, developed and agreed by senior managers from all services involved. The vision is translated into realistic children's centre goals and common targets, supplemented by statements of the principles and values of the children's centre.

Table 1.5 Children's centre offer

CHILDREN'S CENTRES – THE OFFER	
30 per cent most disadvantaged areas	**In less disadvantaged areas**
■ Integrated childcare and early learning ■ Child and family health services ■ Parenting and family support ■ Outreach and home visiting ■ Links with Jobcentre Plus ■ Support for childminders ■ Support for children and parents with special educational needs	■ Drop-in sessions and activities for children parents/carers ■ Child and family health services ■ Parenting and family support ■ Outreach and home visiting ■ Links with Jobcentre Plus ■ Support for childminders ■ Support for children and parents with special educational needs

The roles and responsibilities of each partner are clearly defined and incorporated into a children's centre agreement that sets out the ground rules. Good multi-agency management requires a strong understanding of the available baseline data, as well as ongoing monitoring to provide a clear view of the scale and nature of the needs of children and families in the local community, in order to inform how they can best be met.

Multi-disciplinary multi-functional services have to be dynamic, in order to respond to the complex, changing and sometimes chaotic circumstances that young children and families experience.

The Director of a children's centre in Kent commented on good integrated multi-agency working:

> When you can hear a community worker, play worker and health visitor discussing plans for a child – no hours on the phone or reams of paperwork – you think, 'Yes', this is the model of practice for the 21st century.
>
> (Sure Start 2006: 13)

Ten Sure Start criteria for successful children's centre collaboration

1. **Establish an environment that supports risk and avoids blame**
2. **Be flexible to meet the real needs of the people services are intended to help**
3. **Take steps to promote a genuinely shared vision for activities among partners**
4. **Remain focused on what you really want to do**
5. **Be sensitive to the ways in which change affects individuals**
6. **Think about sustainability from the start. Introduce charges, however small, from day one for services**
7. **Involve parents at all levels**
8. **Build relationships with key people**
9. **Build on what you do well**
10. **Identify shared targets and areas of mutual interest to promote partnership**

(NCSL 2006b: 17)

The government's expectations for children's centres

By 2008, 2,500 children's centres will be operational, largely in the most deprived areas.

By 2010, there will be 3,500 centres (one for every community) in England. Seventy per cent of children's centres will be co-located with primary schools.

Further activities for school leaders and heads of children's centres

The following questions, based on aspects covered in this chapter related to the development of extended schools and children's centres, will enable you to discuss and identify ways forward in meeting the government's change for children agenda.

- How will you ensure you provide the services the community needs?
- What more could you realistically provide in addition to the current offer?
- Who do you need to work with most closely in order to ensure service provision is most effective?
- What further practical steps do you need to take in order to engage with other local schools/centres?
- What barriers are hindering the provision of some services, and how could these be overcome?
- How can you involve those from external agencies and other organisations in the planning and development process?

2

Benefits and Challenges of Extended Schools and Children's Centres

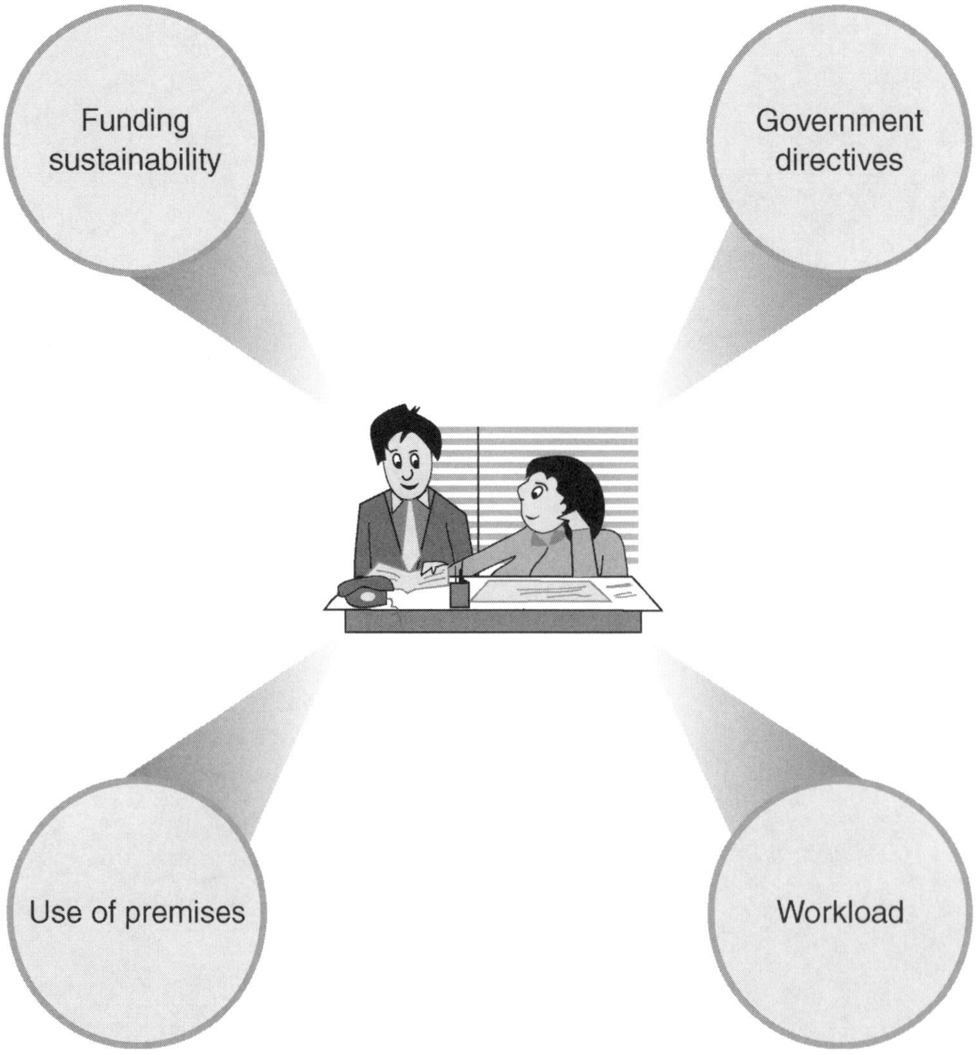

Vision versus reality

Sure Start children's centres are opening at a pace across the country. Extended schools are developing more gradually, as the complexities of workforce remodelling and single status agreement begin to unfold. The government's relentless pace of change and compulsion on school leaders is beginning to take its toll. This is evident by the difficulties in recruiting headteachers.

Like it or not, the government expects that all schools will be an extended school offering 'dawn to dusk' childcare provision for children aged 3 to 14, by 2010. This vision and expectation has already raised some reservations among headteachers.

Sue Kirkham, President of the Association of School and College Leaders (ASCL), commented in June 2006 that:

> There are huge potential pitfalls in expanding extended school services to the level the government has indicated. There is still insufficient clarity about funding, charging for activities and the roles of school leaders and governors. . . . The funding currently committed to extended schools . . . is inadequate in the long-term.

The National Association of Headteachers (NAHT) have equally expressed concerns about the extended school initiative in relation to childcare provision. They consider there is a real danger that the 'dawn to dusk' childcare provision may actually destroy and detract from family values, by children's needs not being met by parents in the home.

Emma Hutchinson (2004), Director of Music House for Children, a charity providing after-school music lessons, expressed her concern that extended schools in the future will create psychological issues for children who spend up to 10 hours a day in school and don't have breakfast or after-school time with their parents.

Bob Holman (2004), a retired community worker in Glasgow, felt that children in school care for 10 hours a day will be even more vulnerable to exhaustion, and that the government should have researched the physical and emotional effects on children of extended service provision, before its launch.

A full-service extended school co-ordinator commented:

> The core offer of 8–6 is there but we know that kids generally don't want to stay that late. They're not wanting to spend their whole lives here.
>
> (DfES 2006c: 60).

Mick Brookes, Chief Executive of the NAHT in 2006 considered that the government is inveigling headteachers to run a 'national babysitting service' at the cost of eroding school leaders' work–life balance and damaging the capacity of schools to fulfil their core purpose. The evidence from a NAHT survey in 2006, also indicated that 27 per cent of headteachers would consider quitting if their workload was not reduced.

According to the Improvement and Development Agency (IDeA):

> extended schools are not resourced to manage the increased administration associated with new responsibilities.
>
> (IDeA 2004: 17)

Steve Sinnott, NUT General Secretary, also expressed the view that the government appears to have moved the goalposts, moving very quickly from the idea of providing services to some of the most vulnerable children, to overall provision for the majority of working parents, which is very different.

Facts and figures about childcare provision

- **UK spending on childcare and early years represents 0.8% of GDP compared to 2–2.5% in Denmark and Sweden.**
- **Childcare and early years commands only 0.78% of total government spending in 2007/08 compared to 5.8% on defence.**
- **There is only one childcare place for every four children currently available.**
- **The typical cost for a full-time nursery place for a child under 2 is £141 a week, £7,300 a year.**
- **The average salary for a childcare worker is £6,100 (at £5.50 an hour), and £11,800 for a senior childcare manager (at £9.66 an hour).**
- **2% of primary schools and 0.5% of secondary schools are providing the full 8a.m. to 6p.m. year round extended schools offer, with 12% and 10% respectively delivering this during term time only.**

(Finch 2006)

Extended schools must meet local need, rather than national compulsion. The extended school initiative clearly challenges and questions existing educational assumptions as to where their focus should be, i.e. the academic achievement of pupils, or the economic productivity of parents.

John Craig suggested:

> The freedom to start from where communities are, rather than where national policy suggests they ought to be, will be crucial to the legitimacy and, ultimately, the success of extended schools.
>
> (Craig *et al.* 2004: 39)

Extended schools and children's centres are good examples of *Every Child Matters* in action, acting as a gateway for this essential strategy. However, headteachers need to be aware that under the Children Act 2004, schools are actually exempt from the legal 'duty to cooperate', which other services (health and social care) must abide by.

However, Clause 36 of the Education and Inspection Act 2006, places a duty on the governing body of all maintained schools to have regard to the relevant local authority Children and Young People's Plan or equivalent, if an excellent local authority, when discharging their functions in relation to the conduct of the school (the traditional teaching and learning side) and when providing services to the community, i.e. extended school services. While headteachers accept the underlying philosophy and concept of extended schools and children's centres, they have deep reservations about the practicalities.

A recent 4Children survey into extended schools (2005) highlighted the main concerns and barriers preventing headteachers from providing childcare and extended school services. These were:

- staffing – make-up and availability of an appropriate Children's Workforce and building capacity;
- premises – availability, access, maintenance and security;
- sustainability of the wider offer of services and activities to families;
- financial and legal responsibilities – sustainability of funding, worries that the headteacher will carry the ultimate responsibility for poor service delivery from other providers, who they commissioned;
- time and workload for leaders and other staff engaged in the initiative;
- lack of sufficient information;
- lack of help from the local authority.

Philippa Thompson from 4Children identified the four biggest challenges for school leaders:

- scale and speed of the extended school development;
- complexity of funding;
- capacity of communities to engage with the initiative and agenda;
- infancy of the extended school model at a strategic level.

(Thompson 2006: 1)

A headteacher from a co-located nursery school and children's centre identified similar problems in relation to staffing and management issues.

- Children's centres are struggling to attract teachers due to the gulf existing between teachers' pay and that of other childcare workers. For example, a qualified teacher can earn more than £30,000 in the classroom, while a nursery nurse earns an average of £14,664 a year.
- Children's centres open for 10 hours a day, 48 weeks a year, when teachers' contracts are for 39 working weeks.
- Qualified teachers who work in a children's centre are entitled to 10 per cent planning, preparation and assessment (PPA) time. Other members of staff who have teaching responsibilities in a centre, i.e. nursery nurses, have no entitlement to non-contact time.
- Managing two budgets is complex, e.g. the nursery school budget and a separate budget for the children's centre provision for the under threes.
- Governance responsibilities – moving from a traditional maintained nursery school governing body to one that is also responsible for the provision in the children's centre is a complex management process.
- The time needed by already fully stretched health or social services professionals working in children's centres, to attend governing body multi-agency committee meetings, outside working hours, is another problematic management aspect.

(*TES* 2006)

Issues for extended schools

Headteachers in the early days of establishing extended service provision identified the following real issues in relation to the practicalities:

- Who gets priority for the use of shared school space – adults or children?
- How long can a school or children's centre sustain providing 'in-kind' costs to cover free tea, coffee, stationery and the use of a telephone?
- Ensuring that school staff are made fully aware on a daily basis of what out-of-school-hours activities are taking place, where, when and with whom.
- The wear and tear and potential loss or breakage to classroom facilities and resources by the multiple use of learning areas.

Tensions can arise when there are two different management and governance systems in operation for a primary school and a co-located children's centre. For example:

- although the two sets of staff work closely together, they do have different conditions of service;
- where a primary school has a maintained nursery this often has to compete with the nursery at the co-located children's centre.

Other tensions can arise:

- where a children's centre is co-located on the same site as a primary school, extra pressure can arise in relation to the use of shared amenities such as car parking and the security of premises.

A north-west headteacher of a co-located primary school and children's centre considers that the issues can be overcome by system leadership that is distributed and goes lateral. In such instances the headteacher of the primary school, as overall head of the school and the children's centre, oversees the entire operation, while the deputy headteacher takes on the school management role, and an assistant head of the school runs the children's centre.

Sustainability, as one area of major concern for school and children's centre leaders, is not just about grants and funding. It is about maintaining interest, encouraging involvement, anticipating and adapting to change and nurturing suitably skilled community volunteers. This is achieved largely through partnership working, networking and moving management of projects to an outside agency.

One head of a children's centre in the north-east considered that:

> Schools focus on the children on their roll, but a children's centre has to cater for an entire neighbourhood, and some of those children go to other schools.
>
> (Revell 2006: 29)

Why participate in the extended school and children's centre agenda?

- We have a moral duty to consider children and young people's rights: children and young people have a right to be heard and play a part in the decisions that affect them (Article 12 of UN Children's Rights Convention);
- to raise standards and meet the *Every Child Matters* outcomes;
- to provide and ensure parental involvement;
- to involve the local community;
- to reduce burdens on teachers.

Myths about extended schools and solutions to dispel the myths

The following table summarises the commonly held myths about extended schools, and offers solutions to dispel each myth.

Table 2.1 Extended school myths

Myth	**Dispelling the myth**
1. **Work overload** – schools have got enough to do without taking on yet another initiative.	Workload will actually decrease as frontline workers from health and social care, independent, voluntary and community organisations support the well-being of children and young people.
2. **Turf** – external agencies should stay where they are and not use the school to offer their service.	Schools can no longer address the well-being problems pupils may face, alone. They need the support and therapeutic interventions of health and social care services to help remove and minimise barriers to learning. More convenient if such services are provided in the school, where children are.
3. **Liability** – increased if school offers services delivered by external providers on their premises.	Properly written multi-agency and partner agreements minimise the school's liability from the start, and ensure responsibility is shared.

Myth	Dispelling the myth
4. **Parental resistance** – to on-site extended school wrap-around care provision. Viewed as interference with family values.	Involvement of parents and family in the planning of provision from the start to give them a sense of ownership and a say in what is needed tends to win support, and foster parent advocates in the community.
5. **Unsuitability** – of extended school initiative in relation to the schools context, e.g. leafy suburbs, little if any social deprivation.	The school should be taking the wider view and looking beyond their own pupil population. The school in partnership with a cluster of other local schools may contribute to providing elements of the core offer across a local networked community.
6. **Diversion** – away from the school's core purpose of teaching and learning.	Achievement and well-being go hand in hand. Any well-being interventions from health and social care complement and contribute to the child's whole curriculum, adopting a holistic approach to meeting the needs of the child.
7. **Responsibility** – why should schools take on the responsibilities of parents, through the provision of extended services and wrap-around care?	Schools are at the heart of the community, acting as service hubs. They are helping parents to take greater interest and responsibility in their child's learning by being able to access a range of services more conveniently on the school site.
8. **Administration** – of extra external staff on the school site puts pressure on school staff amenities as well as causing confusion about roles.	Cross-training programme for school and multi-agency staff will help to clarify roles. Enhancing staff facilities and amenities.
9. **Discrimination** – school staff may have concerns about those with mental health or drug abuse problems from the community accessing health care services on the same site where children are being educated.	Remind staff about the moral purpose, i.e. we all have a right to achieve and fulfil our potential and have a second chance in life. Everyone in this community matters.

The benefits of extended schools and children's centres

It is still too early to really judge the benefits of extended schools and children's centres on children, young people and families. Anne Longfield, Chief Executive of the charity 4Children acknowledged that until hard outcomes data becomes available, the case for the agenda remains one of assertion. DfES research (2005g), revealed only anecdotal evidence relating to the potential positive outcomes of extended schools. These included raised pupil attainment, increased pupil engagement with learning and growing trust and support between families and schools. Similarly, OFSTED in their HMI report published in July 2006, identified the major benefits to children, young people and adults of extended services as resulting in:

> enhanced self-confidence, improved relationships, raised aspirations and better attitudes to learning
>
> (OFSTED 2006c: 3)

The DfES, in their research brief published in September 2006, confirmed the benefits of full service extended schools in terms of improvements on performance measures (such as student attainment and exclusion rates) and increased intake numbers.

Where multi-agency services are co-located with schools, collaborative working brings the benefits of shared information and resources, proactive and earlier intervention, reduced time in making referrals and following up on cases and the harnessing of talents from different professionals.

The following table highlights the benefits of extended schools and children's centres for a range of stakeholders.

Table 2.2 The benefits of extended schools and children's centres

Benefits for children and young people
■ Contribute to meeting the *Every Child Matters* five outcomes ■ Sharper focus on meeting children and young people's needs ■ Higher levels of attendance ■ Increased motivation and self-esteem ■ Specialist support to meet children and young people's wider needs by placing them at the centre of a network of services which supports their learning and well-being ■ Access to additional facilities and equipment to enhance learning ■ Enables children and young people to have fun and develop wider interests and new skills ■ Improved attitudes to learning ■ Higher levels of achievement in the longer term ■ Growing up in a community where learning is valued ■ Greater personalisation ■ More opportunities for gifted and talented and SEN children and young people, helping to close the achievement gap ■ Enhances support for vulnerable children and young people, and those at risk ■ Promotes equality of opportunity for children and young people to participate in a wide range of activities
Benefits for staff
■ Provides better opportunities for flexible working and career development ■ Provides easier access to essential services for staff, helping staff recruitment and retention ■ Provides better help for staff to address children and young people's wider needs through the support of multi-agency frontline workers
Benefits for parents/carers and families
■ Provides better help to parents to address children's wider needs, such as support from visiting multi-agency teams ■ Ensures greater availability of specialist support services in their neighbourhood ■ Encourages greater parental involvement in children's learning, behaviour and well-being ■ Re-engages adults with education and creates local learning and job opportunities, enabling parents to return to work, thus reducing the number of children living in poverty ■ Reduces health inequality through greater take up of school-based health and social care services by families ■ Develops increased trust and support between families and school/children's centre
Benefits for the community
■ Increased responsiveness to community needs ■ Increases community pride and aspirations through involvement

■ Better access to essential specialist services ■ Improved local availability of sports, arts, libraries and other facilities ■ Opportunities for intergenerational initiatives and learning ■ Better supervision of children outside school hours ■ Reinvigorates and regenerates local communities ■ Reduces levels of anti-social behaviour ■ Makes better use of resources ■ Provides local career development opportunities ■ Promotes better relationships and enhanced partnership working with the school/children's centre
Benefits for partner external and supporting multi-agencies
■ Service delivery in the heart of the community ■ More effective engagement with clients ■ Better and improved communication between agencies, resulting in more efficient and effective service provision ■ Reduced time in making referrals and in following up cases ■ Better value for money

Source: DfES (2002a) *An Introduction: Extended Schools providing Opportunities and Services for All.* London: Department for Education and Skills.

The Chief HMI in a conference speech in March 2006 shared an example with delegates where extended school provision had been of great benefit to a pupil and his family:

> In a secondary school, a boy in Year 8 spoke of the problems he and his family had experienced and how help from services based in the school had supported them all. His father felt that without this his son would have stopped attending school.
>
> (OFSTED 2006a: 6–7)

The challenges for extended schools, with practical solutions

Extended schools, more than children's centres, face immense challenges in developing extended school provision. These are illustrated in the following table. Possible solutions, based on best-practice experience from mainstream and special schools, are offered.

Table 2.3 Challenges for extended schools with solutions

Nature of challenge	Recommended solutions
Under-use and low take-up of extended school activities	Opening at weekends and in school holidays; increased promotion of activities and services in local community; ensuring provision matches local needs
Parochial loyalties prevailing which affect governance	Increase opportunities for collaboration involving governors with other partners; enhance school site-based decision making opportunities
Funding for sustainability	Seek new opportunities to attract additional funding – writing and submitting bid proposals; charging for some extended services; deciding what to subsidise; seeking local business and charitable sponsorship

Table 2.3 *(Continued)*

Nature of challenge	Recommended solutions
Training for new ways of working and capacity building	Engage in cross-agency, cross-school cluster joint training programmes focused on developing new skills and knowledge for delivering and implementing *Every Child Matters*, to equip a Children's Workforce, to familiarise staff with the use of the common assessment framework
Resistance and reluctance to changing the use of school premises by other providers	Regular ongoing, clear information dissemination about the reasons for change, openly communicated to stakeholders
Differences in aims, cultures and procedures between schools and other partner agencies	Use of common language, clarity of roles made explicit, working to consistent agreed frameworks and protocols
Work overload	Appoint a dedicated extended school co-ordinator and ensure job description allows for sufficient time to perform extensive role; create opportunities for other staff to participate – distributed leadership
Complexity of competing priorities	Planning adequate lead-in time prior to extended school service delivery; adopting stepped change; implementing a few activities and priorities well
Gender imbalances in participation in extended school activities by adults	Providing activities and programmes to engage fathers in their child's learning, e.g. sessions just for fathers together; activities led by male tutor or support worker
Lack of engagement in extended school activities by pupils and parents living in outlying parts of the school's catchments	Negotiate sharing another school's minibus; negotiate with public transport companies for extending services in out-of-school hours; explore what other schools have to offer nearer to where parents/pupils live
Open to legal challenge and liability if activities and services go wrong or don't match up to users expectations (litigation culture)	Checking the policy and public liability of any partner or organisation delivering services and activities, before agreeing to allow them to deliver provision on the premises
Competing local priorities and conflicts of interest, e.g. raising standards of achievement, versus reducing teenage pregnancy or drug misuse	Making the *Every Child Matters* outcomes explicit to stakeholders and the local community, taking the wider community view and sharing this vision via the Mission Statement
Poor perception of the school in the local community due to a deficit view, e.g. stigmatised as a result of being associated with problem families and problem children	Raising the profile of the organisation through positive marketing of the value of the school/centre and its related services in addressing the needs of the community, as identified by them, i.e. press releases, newsletters, local radio coverage, displays in local library or community centre

Table 2.3 *(Continued)*

Nature of challenge	Recommended solutions
Ensuring that extended services and activities can be sustained, especially where socially deprived families don't have sufficient money to pay for services and activities	Building in contingency funding and the capacity to subsidise, if necessary, some activities and services for the most needy families and pupils, from profits made from charging for other community activities
Potential staffing tensions between teachers and multi-agency frontline workers, due to different working relationships with children and young people	Making explicit the role and remit of teaching staff and frontline workers from multi-agencies and how each contributes to the well-being and removal of barriers to learning of the children and young people they work with
School/children's centre have the monopoly of local service provision, which has resulted in the closure of some other local community facilities	Engaging the support of the local authority in justifying to local community members why some services or public facilities have been relocated at the school or children's centre
Some families and community members actively opting not to access services on school premises due to their own past negative experiences of schooling	Using advocates and informal showcase celebration or open day events, coffee mornings to publicise first hand the value and enjoyment gained from the services and activities on offer for families and the community
Concerns about potential selectivity existing in some schools such as academies or specialist schools, despite government changes to admissions policies, which disadvantage the local 'less desirable' groups of pupils and their families from accessing a good range of services	Parental choice, equal opportunities and inclusion policies being made explicit and challenged, where necessary

OFSTED (2006c) identified the lack of continuity in the provision of support services and interventions between children's centres and schools, especially when children moved from the centre on to a school. Local authorities can best address this issue as part of their cross-phase strategy for improving transfer and transition.

There is no doubt that extended schools and children's centres bring a radical shift in thinking, working within and beyond the standards agenda, to build capacity and make a difference locally.

Further activities for school leaders and heads of children's centres

The following questions are designed to enable you to discuss and identify the positive ways forward in meeting the challenges posed by the development of extended schools and children's centres.

- How can you learn about extended schooling and children's centres and share this knowledge effectively with key stakeholders?
- In the context of your community, why do you want to become an extended school?
- What is the scope of your ambition to become an extended school or children's centre?
- What are the views of the whole staff to the extended school and/or children's centre initiative?

- What are the local political risks of extended schooling and/or children's centre provision, and how can these be pre-empted and managed?
- How can you ensure and demonstrate the legitimacy of the move to developing and enhancing extended service provision?
- What is needed to make the extended school and/or children's centre initiative happen successfully in your setting?
- How will the organisation, parents and the community avoid developing a deficit view about the extended school and/or children's centre initiative?
- What will be the benefit to children, young people and families in the community as a result of the extended school/children's centre services you provide?

3

How to Set Up and Run Effective Extended School Service Provision

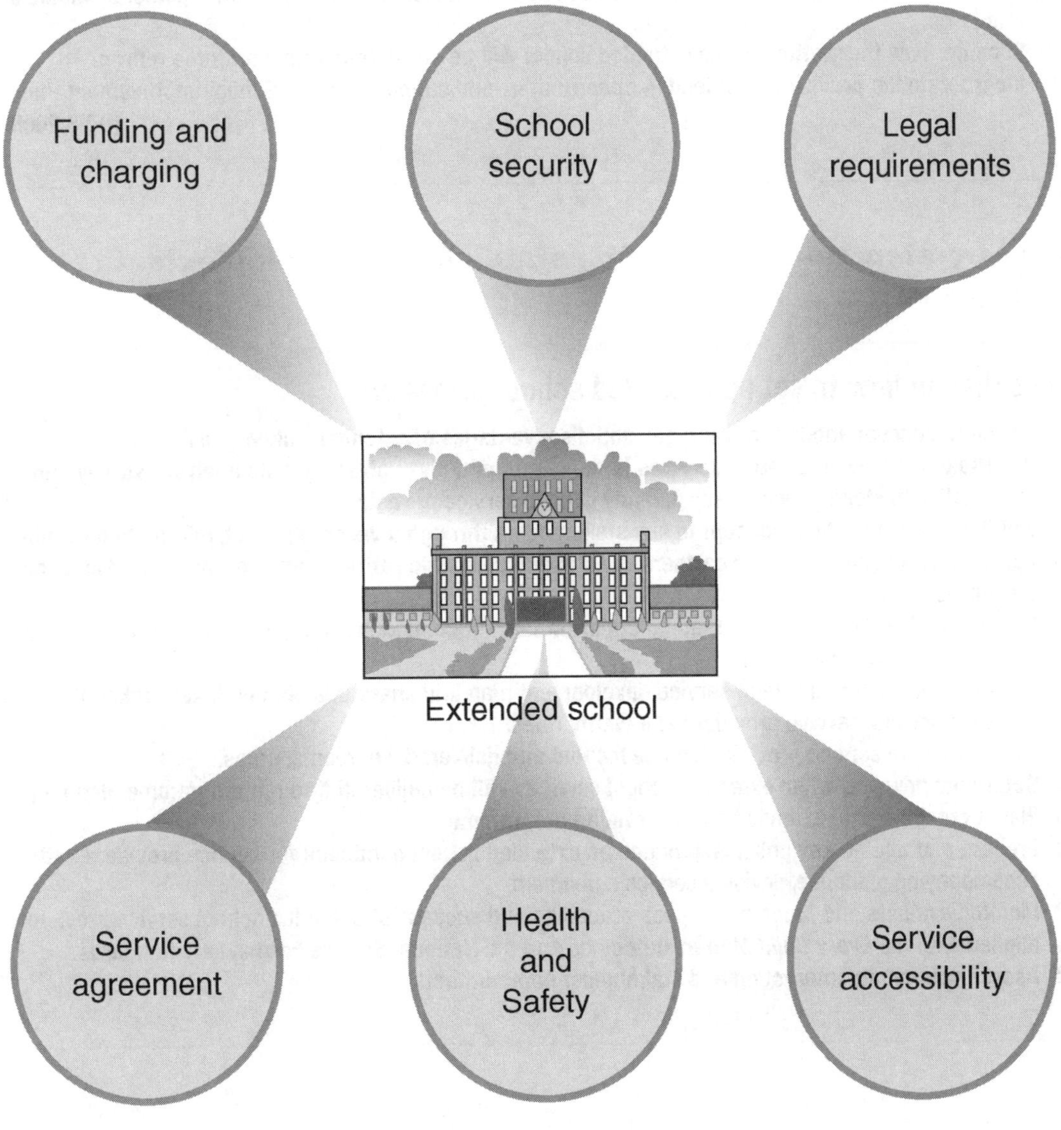

Checklist for schools planning to offer extended activities

1. Read the contents of the DfES guidance on *Planning and Funding Extended Schools* (issued June 2006), and the ContinYou/DfES Know-how series of leaflets on the Teachernet website.
2. Contact the local authority's extended schools remodelling adviser (ESRA).
3. Review existing local provision, with the help of the ESRA.
4. Consider any particular local challenges, such as rurality, which might require special transport or other arrangements.
5. Look at good practice examples from other schools and communities.
6. Consult with the school's governing body on the best way forward.
7. Consult with school staff, their professional associations and unions, and any existing collaborative partners.
8. Decide how to consult effectively with children and young people, their families and the wider community.
9. Set up ongoing consultation on the extended opportunities needed by pupils, families and the local community, particularly the most vulnerable and disadvantaged.
10. Identify the skills and resources available to help in the local community and amongst local partner providers, and build partnerships with them.
11. Work with all parents and other stakeholders to identify affordable charges which will help to make extended opportunities sustainable.
12. Define (through the governing body) when and how remission from charging arrangements should come into force.
13. Consider how the staffing of the extended school will be consistent with workforce reform.
14. Incorporate the provision of extended opportunities and support into the School Improvement Plan.

(DfES 2006b: 9)

A step-by-step guide on how to establish and develop extended school provision

Checklist on how to set up extended school provision

- ❑ Research concept, models, advantages and disadvantages of extended school provision.
- ❑ Undertake a review of existing services in the community through audit, data analysis, survey and consultation to identify local needs and any gaps in service provision.
- ❑ Sell the extended school concept to key stakeholders through a visioning event, information evening.
- ❑ Agree a few specific goals with partners and stakeholders which are sustainable, and support and underpin the mission statement.
- ❑ Identify funding streams, seek funding opportunities – income generating, sponsorship, writing bid proposals and a business plan.
- ❑ Construct an extended school service development plan and share this plan with key stakeholders.
- ❑ Identify partners, service providers and clarify roles.
- ❑ Map out where service provision will be located and delivered, i.e. rooms, areas.
- ❑ Determine how and when extended school services will be delivered through programme planning.
- ❑ Plan a cross-service extended school training programme.
- ❑ Prepare and update key policies, produce an extended school handbook for service providers with accompanying guidance, devise a service agreement.
- ❑ Monitor, evaluate and judge the impact, outcomes and success of extended school service provision, aligned with the *Every Child Matters* outcomes and the National Service Framework standards.
- ❑ Assess community interaction and stakeholder commitment.

Operational aspects

This chapter will cover operational aspects, legal requirements and the practicalities of extended school provision. It complements and reflects the information provided in the ContinYou/DfES 'know how' leaflets.

Basic principles of funding and charging for extended school services

Checklist for funding and charging for extended school services

- ❑ **Keep separate accounts distinct from the school's delegated budget for additional activities and services for the community.**
- ❑ **Ensure extended school community activities are self-financing. (Study support is the only exception.)**
- ❑ **Ensure pupils are not charged for education outside school hours if it is part of the National Curriculum, preparation for an exam or part of Religious Education (RE).**
- ❑ **There must be an extended school statement of general policy on charging in place before charges for participation in community activities or services at the school are requested.**
- ❑ **Where voluntary contributions for some extended school activities are requested from community members and parents, it must be made clear how such contributions will be used.**
- ❑ **Where a large programme of extended services and activities are being offered, it is recommended that the school employs an independent adviser to help them develop a business plan.**
- ❑ **Funding must be used for the specific service provision it was intended for, e.g. Learning and Skills Council (LSC) funding for adult education classes.**
- ❑ **Take into account that some extended school services and activities may be subject to VAT.**
- ❑ **Charging fees must cover additional costs for the use of premises, utility services, cleaning and maintenance, refreshments, caretaker, security, equipment hire, administration, staffing, insurance.**
- ❑ **Support other extended school activities and services from income generated through charging for some activities.**
- ❑ **Don't rely too much on discretionary funding for extended school activities as this will become increasingly more difficult to acquire, as more extended schools in the area develop their provision.**
- ❑ **If there is any failure to comply with the regulations on financial procedures then the governing body's power to discharge the delegated budget will be removed.**
- ❑ **Where you are uncertain about funding any aspect of extended school provision, seek further guidance from the local authority (LA) financial services. There is specific LA guidance on financing community activities.**

Charging for extended school activities

Schools directly providing extended activities must comply with legislation.

- The governing body must devise and publish a charging and fee remission policy, in consultation with parents.
- A school cannot make any charges to parents unless this policy exists.
- Any profits made from extended activities must be reinvested in the school/service.
- Schools may use their delegated budgets to subsidise a child's access to chargeable extended activities where they consider that the activities are provided for the purposes of the school, because they are of educational benefit to the child.
- Schools may not charge for any study support activities provided during the school day, except for music tuition, or for provision before or after the school day, which deliver the National Curriculum or prepare a child for a public examination.
- Schools may lawfully charge for other study support, e.g. additional sport, drama and music clubs, holiday activities, visits and additional courses, such as first aid, following consultation.

The government guidance (2006) provides examples on when and when not to charge for extended school activities.

Extended activities to be charged at full cost

- Breakfast club
- After-school childcare

Charges imposed to cover costs

- Foreign language clubs
- Local history clubs
- Photography clubs

Extended activities to be offered free of charge

- Catch-up maths and literacy club and stretch activities for gifted and talented
- Easter revision week for GCSE students
- Extra Science tuition for under performing children
- Extra lessons for underachieving groups, such as children in public care.

(DfES 2006b)

Mick Brookes, General Secretary of the NAHT, considered that it would become problematic and an administrative nightmare for schools when drawing a distinction between activities that were to be charged for and those that were to be free. For example, a pupil could be charged for staying on for the after-school football club or foreign language club, but would not be charged to attend the reading club or the maths 'catch-up' club.

John Dunford, the General Secretary of the Secondary Heads Association, considered it would become difficult for schools and confusing for parents as children in one room would be doing an extra-curricular activity free, while children in the next room could be doing another activity which has to be paid for.

Chris Keates, General Secretary of the National Association of School Masters and Union of Women Teachers (NASUWT), considered local authorities should set out benchmark costs to help schools know what it is reasonable to charge. She was concerned that if schools made a profit from charging for an activity, then the profit may distract from the prime focus on learning.

How much to charge

Government guidance on the extended schools programme suggests that schools could charge as much as £70 a week during term time and £200 a week during the holidays for out-of-school-hours activities, with charges working out at an average of £4 to £4.50 an hour.

However, costs can vary widely, depending on the locality the school is situated in, the raw materials required such as healthy food for a breakfast club, the cost of staff time to run the club, administration overheads and rent. The charge to a child for attending a breakfast club may vary from 50 p to £2.00 per session. Charges for Easter or summer holiday play schemes can cost up to £15 a day for the first child in a family, £12 for the second child and £10 for the third child. After-school club activities run during term time covering a range of sports, arts and crafts, drama, music and computers can cost on average £7 per session for the first child in a family, £5 for the second child and £4 for the third child. An after-school club cost may in some instances include a meal and minibus collection of children attending from other local schools. A 90-minute after-school art club session for a full term can cost £56 per child. Day childcare provision can cost £4.19 per hour for a child under two, and £3.78 per hour for older children. This is expensive, particularly for parents who may have more than one child attending out-of-school-hours activities.

Extended schools do offer subsidised places on application determined by need, and working parents on lower incomes can reclaim 80 per cent of costs back from the childcare element of the

Working Tax Credit. The government measure of poverty is 'living below sixty per cent of the median income', i.e. living on an income of less than £175 per week.

Low-income families and lone parents can claim for assistance with childcare costs of up to £175 a week for one child and £300 a week for two or more children, if one or both parents work at least 16 hours a week. This means that they can receive up to a maximum of £140 per week for one child and £240 per week where there are two children. Unemployed parents cannot reclaim childcare costs. In the case of a one-child family on an annual income of £30,000 they could claim up to £4,435 through the childcare element of the Working Tax Credit. Some parents may value help and advice on how to complete Part 3 of the Tax Credit claim form to enable them to recoup childcare costs. One school, as part of its extended provision core offer, employed an education social worker to support this aspect. Further information about the Tax Credit claim form can be found at www.hmrc.gov.uk/taxcredits or on 0845 300 3900.

Sources of funding for extended school provision

Funding sources will vary from school to school, depending on the types of services being offered and the local context. While none of the funding for extended schools is ring-fenced, the government is encouraging schools to earmark the money for extended schooling and personalised learning.

Funding streams available

Funding earmarked for schools:

- **School Standards Grant (SSG) – school flexibility about focus of the spend.**
- **School Standards Grant (personalisation) to support access to extended activities, e.g. 'catch up' intervention support in literacy and numeracy, Gifted and Talented provision.**
- **Dedicated School Grant (personalisation) for schools serving areas of high deprivation, which can be used for extended activities.**

Funding via local authority to start up extended services:

- **Standards Fund: Revenue (SF106)**
- **General Sure Start Grant: Revenue**
- **General Sure Start Grant: Capital**

{ for the development of childcare services and other activities, integrated services or young children and their families.

Other sources of funding:

- **Early Years Development and Childcare Partnerships funding**
- **Specialist Schools and Colleges funding**
- **Children's Centres Capital and Revenue funds**
- **Children's Trusts funding**
- **The Learning and Skills Council funding**
- **Physical Education, School Sport and Club Links Strategy (PESSCL) funding**
- **Neighbourhood Renewal funding**
- **Children's Fund**
- **European Social Fund**
- **Lottery funding**
- **Charitable grants and donations from private sponsors**

For further information about funding download: *Planning and Funding Extended Schools: A Guide for Schools, Local Authorities and their Partner Organisations* from: www.teachernet.gov.uk/extendedschools and the document on value for money from www.dfes.gov.uk/valueformoney/docs/VFM_Document_405.doc. It is also useful to make reference to the ContinYou guidance (2005a) entitled *Fundraising Guidance. Study Support/Out-of-school-hours Learning (oshl).*

Model Charging and Remission Policy for Extended School Activities

Introduction
This document sets out the policy for the charging and remission of school activities taking place both within and outside school hours. The policy is kept under annual review in line with the priorities on the school development plan. It conforms to the charging and remission policy of the local authority.

Purpose
The policy informs parents/carers, families, members of the community and school staff about charging for school activities.

Aims
The policy aims to:
- follow the basic principle that education is free of charge if it is connected with the National Curriculum, or Statutory Religious Education taught at the school, or related to a prescribed public examination;
- make no charge for equipment, books, materials and transportation related to the delivery of the National Curriculum, statutory Religious Education or for a prescribed public examination.

Responsibilities
The Governing Body of the school, in consultation with the headteacher, are responsible for the implementation of this policy.

Residential activities
No charge is made for the education or the cost of travel for a residential activity taking place during school time, or essential to the education provided at the school.

Charges can be made however for board and lodging in relation to residential activities, except for pupils whose parents are receiving income support, income-based job seekers allowance or family tax credit.

A trip falls within school time if the number of school sessions missed by the pupils amounts to half or more of the number of days taken up by the activity. Each school day is normally divided into two sessions and each 24-hour period is divided into two half days beginning at noon and midnight.

For example, a term-time trip from noon on Wednesday to 9pm on Sunday, would last for nine half-days including five school sessions, and would count as taking place in school time. A trip from noon on Thursday to 9pm on Sunday would count as seven half-days, including three school sessions, and would therefore be classified for charging purposes, as taking place outside school-time.

Where an activity is classified for charging purposes as taking place outside school time and not essential to the education provided at the school, it will be open to all pupils regardless of their parents ability or willingness to pay. In these cases, a voluntary contribution will be sought from parents. If the voluntary contributions fail to cover the whole cost of that activity, then it may not take place.

Out of school hours extended school activities
No charge is made for out of school hours learning activities that are specifically related to the National Curriculum, Religious Education, or for a prescribed public examination, e.g. study support.

Parents may be charged for optional extra activities outside school hours which includes: pupil's travel costs; a pupil's board and lodging costs; materials, books, instruments and other equipment; non-teaching staff costs; entrance fees to museums, galleries, castles, theatres; insurance costs. Participation in such optional extra activities are based on parental choice and their willingness to meet such charges as may be made.

Voluntary contributions
The school may invite parents to make a voluntary contribution for their child participating in out of school hours activities. Where a parental contribution is necessary for an activity to take place, this will be fully explained to parents during the activity planning stage. No pupil will be left out of an activity where their parents are unable to make a financial contribution of any kind.

The terms of any request for contributions will be clear:

a) that there is no obligation to contribute; and
b) that registered pupils at the school will not be treated differently according to whether or not their parents have made any contribution.

Voluntary contributions from parents for out of school hours learning activities may include the cost of subsidising pupils from low-income families or the cost of travel for accompanying adults. Parents may be asked to contribute towards part of the cost with the remainder being met from general fund raising events. Where voluntary contributions to an activity result in a surplus of monies over and above the cost of the activity, the surplus will be placed in the school fund to support other activities.

Music tuition
Charges are made in respect of individual or small group tuition in the playing of a musical instrument or tuition in singing, within or outside school hours, when it is not part of a syllabus for a prescribed public examination or related to the National Curriculum. Parental agreement will be sought in advance of any musical instrument or voice tuition taking place.

Public examinations
No charge is made for prescribed public examinations for which registered pupils are being prepared at the school. Where a pupil re-sits an examination and the school has not provided additional preparation, parents will be charged the full costs for entering their child. In the instance where parents request an examination remark, the resulting charge of the examining board may be passed on to parents. If a pupil is entered with parental approval for a public examination not on the prescribed list, a charge will be made for the entry fee. In the instances where a pupil fails to complete examination course work or to sit the final public examination, without good reason, parents will be requested to pay the examination fee.

Other charges

Breakages and fines
Parents are requested to make a contribution towards replacing damaged or lost school property, i.e. a broken window, or a damaged or lost text book, where this is the result of their child's behaviour.

Copying documentation
Parents will be charged for the copying of any requested document, based on a standard charge of 5 pence per page.

Remissions Policy
If a pupil is unable to participate in a school trip because of illness, parents may receive a refund where they have contributed voluntarily. Parents on income support, income-based job seekers allowance or family tax credit will be exempt from charges for their child's board and lodging on a residential education trip.

A sub-committee of the Governing Body with the headteacher will consider each individual pupil case of genuine financial hardship, to support them in participating in chargeable school activities.

This policy was issued on September 2006

The policy will be reviewed and up-dated where necessary, annually.

Figure 3.1 Model Charging and Remission Policy

Details about obtaining this guidance can be found on the ContinYou website www.continyou.org.uk

Cameo of school funding and income generating for extended services

An extended secondary school in the East Riding of Yorkshire raised funds for a new sports complex from various sources which included the local authority, the Football Foundation and a series of concerts held over a three-year period.

This enabled the school to offer adult fitness classes, school swimming lessons and children's parties, and for the sports complex to remain open throughout the school holidays.

Prior to the sports complex being built, the school kitchen had been making a loss. However, since the sports complex has been open, the school kitchen provides three meals a day to cater for sports centre clients as well as pupils, and the profits from the catering are ploughed back into the school.

The income generated from the external facilities cross-subsidises the school. The extra staff employed to provide activities, such as lifeguards, a training manager and a sports centre manager are paid for out of the income generated by their activities.

The headteacher at the same school ensures that while he/she is on the premises, any complaints about extended services are referred to them and dealt with by them. In addition, he/she has established a code of conduct and disciplinary procedures for **any** staff working on the school premises (Leney 2006: 27).

Financial management and sustainable funding for extended school activities

The government guidance issued in June 2006, on planning and funding extended schools, provided helpful advice on financial management and sustainable funding. The guidance clarified how schools could and should use their delegated budgets and report on income and expenditure on extended activities. The table below summarises this.

Table 3.1 Expectations of extended school use of delegated budget

Schools can:	**Schools should:**
▪ Use their delegated budgets to support/subsidise extended activities that bring an educational benefit to children but **not** those such as sports activities solely for the benefit of the community ▪ Use their School Standards Grant to support the full range of extended activities ▪ Report income and expenditure on extended activities that have an educational benefit alongside core school activities	▪ Have a clear understanding of the ongoing costs of delivering extended activities, and how they will be funded ▪ Report separately income and expenditure on community facility activities ▪ Seek the advice of their LA on accounting procedures, and on VAT ▪ Consult the Financial Management Standard website and toolkit to ensure that systems are fit for purpose

Source: DfES 2006b, *Planning and Funding Extended Schools: A Guide for Schools, Local Authorities and their Partner Organisations.* London: Department for Education and Skills.

Use of delegated budgets

A school's delegated budget ('budget share') is the funding schools receive from the LA for the 'purposes of the school' which is construed as embracing all activities that bring an educational benefit to pupils at the school, or to pupils registered at other maintained schools, and which could include activities within childcare. It covers all the teaching and learning activities that schools are required to deliver.

Activities that are not for the 'purposes of the school' and which cannot be funded from the school's delegated budget include the provision of community facilities. The only exception is maintained nursery schools, where schools may fund community facilities, including childcare, from their delegated budget.

To help school leaders decide whether a particular extended activity is eligible to be funded from the delegated budget, refer to the flow diagram below.

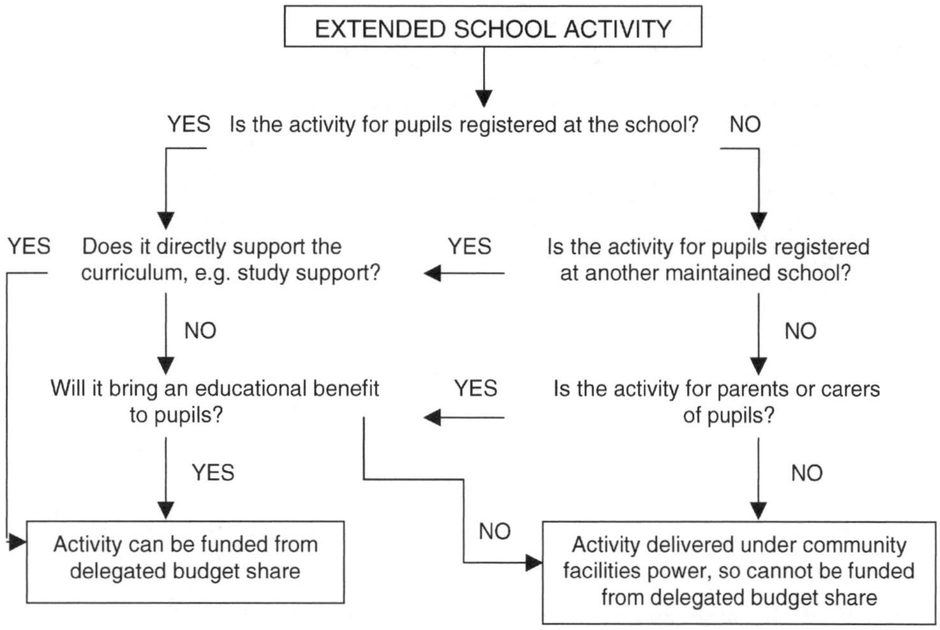

Figure 3.2 Extended school flow diagram to identify if activity is eligible for delegated budget funding. Source: DfES (2006b) *Planning and Funding Extended Schools: A Guide for Schools, Local Authorities and their Partner Organisations.* London: Department for Education and Skills.

After answering the questions on the flow diagram school leaders will be able to clarify if the extended activity can be funded legitimately from the delegated budget. The following examples should help to demystify any uncertainty.

1 A parenting class helps pupils' parents/carers to support their learning – this is eligible for delegated budget funding.
2 A term-time breakfast club for children ensures pupils are in class on time and ready to learn – this is eligible for delegated budget funding.
3 A summer-holiday play scheme with the purpose of childcare acting as a community facility is not eligible for delegated budget funding.

However, a school can purchase a place for an educational trip to a museum within that holiday programme for a child, using its delegated budget funding.

Accounting procedures for extended school activities

The Extended School Remodelling Adviser (ESRA) and the LA finance officer can advise on appropriate accounting arrangements. Depending on the extent and range of extended school activities, it may be advisable to have a free-standing separate bank account, particularly where activities are significant. The school needs to ensure that its accounting procedures can distinguish between those extended school activities that can be funded from the delegated budget, and those that must be funded from outside it.

Management of extended activity finances

School leaders and the governing body need to ensure that they:

- can demonstrate a clear audit trail confirming decisions to undertake individual extended activities and their sources of funding, including whether such activities are eligible/ineligible for delegated budget funds;
- have a robust process for fully costing all extended activities, including the apportionment of the school's fixed costs or overheads as well as the identification of direct costs;
- have all the appropriate systems, processes and controls in place to support a robust charging regime.

Further information can be found on the following website:
www.teachernet.gov.uk/management/schoolfunding/schoolfinance

VAT and extended school activities

Recovering VAT – the provision of most childcare and some extended school services are classed as exempt business activities for VAT purposes. Any VAT incurred in service delivery cannot be passed on to the end user. Input VAT is not recoverable, where the governing body of a LA-maintained school provides extended school activities in its own right, and therefore keeps the generated income. However, if the LA generates and keeps such income, via the 5 per cent VAT recovery route, they may be able to recover any VAT incurred. Childcare-based extended service may be treated as a non-business activity for VAT purposes by the LA.

VAT on the supply of staff providing extended school services – where foundation and voluntary-aided (VA) schools require additional staff to deliver extended school services and the LA provides the staff, that is a supply for VAT purposes. Where voluntary-controlled (VC) and community schools operate extended school services and the governing body appoints additional staff to run activities, the LA is technically the employer of those staff. Any payments made to the LA by the governing body of these schools for the use of these staff in extended school activities is non-business income, and is therefore not subject to VAT.

All other goods and services provided to the governing bodies of VA, VC, foundation and community schools by LAs are subject to VAT at the appropriate rate.

Where some extended services may be provided by third-party contractors, the VAT liability will be dependent on the nature of the services provided. VAT in such instances would not be an issue because the contractors would employ their own staff. If the third-party contractors charge the LA or the governing body of the extended school for their services, which would include overhead costs, i.e. staff wages, these payments would be subject to VAT at the appropriate rate and liability. Depending on the nature of the agreement, the third-party contractor may be charged rent for using the school's buildings, and this charge may be subject to VAT.

Staffing costs may be liable to VAT where LA-employed staff are seconded to work for extended services provided by a contractor. If staff have contracts of employment or letters of appointment that specify the names of joint employers, there is no supply of staff for VAT purposes between them.

Paymaster services for associated companies – these services arise where:

1. one company of jointly employed employees agrees to pay all salaries, national insurance (NI) and pension contributions, which are recovered from the other employer.
2. a number of associated companies employs its own staff, but one (paymaster) company pays all salaries, NI and pension contributions on behalf of the others. Each associate pays its share of the costs to the paymaster.

Recovery of monies paid out by the paymaster in either case is not subject to VAT as it is a disbursement. If a charge is made for the paymaster's services to the other companies over and above the reimbursement of the costs paid out on their behalf, the paymaster must account for VAT on his charge. However, such supplies are disregarded where they are made between companies within the same VAT group registration.

Always seek guidance from your LA financial officer and from www.hmce.gov.uk

Download ContinYou/DfES leaflet *Accounting for VAT* from following website: www.teachernet.gov.uk/wholeschool/extendedschools/practicalknowhow

Table 3.2 Framework for planning an extended school activity

WHO	WHAT
■ wants the activity? ■ is responsible for planning and updating the activity? (Involve the pupils) ■ is the activity for? (specific age group, poor readers, gifted and talented) ■ can attend the club? (parents, grandparents, siblings) ■ is going to staff the activity? (school staff, volunteers, external provider) ■ else can help? (police, PCT, community groups, college, university) ■ is going to write any letters or complete any funding bid forms?	■ activity(s) are you going to run? ■ are you going to call the club? ■ paperwork do you need? e.g. register, code of conduct forms, parental audits, pupil surveys ■ are you going to do if demand outstrips supply? ■ will the activity/club achieve? ■ other similar activities/clubs are running locally that could compete?
WHERE	**WHEN**
■ are you intending to deliver the activity? ■ will you get any volunteers to help run the activity from? ■ will you apply for additional funding or sponsorship if required?	■ are you going to start the activity? (Remember it takes up to 3 months to know the outcome of any financial bid, to run the club/activity)
WHY	**HOW**
■ are you wanting to run the activity/club? (to improve the behaviour, motivation, attitude, self-esteem of young people; to reduce lateness, increase social skills; support local families, provide childcare)	■ are you going to publicise the activity/club? (newsletter, posters) ■ is the activity going to be totally different from the curriculum? (interesting, fun, exciting) ■ will you know the activity/club has been a success? ■ are you going to encourage attendance at the activity/club? (reward certificates for good attendance) ■ how much is it going to cost to run the activity?

Table 3.2 *(Continued)*

HOW MUCH – COST
■ staffing (number of hours × weeks × pay rate) ■ rental/hire of any premises, specialist facilities ■ transport ■ refreshments ■ resources ■ in-kind donations, e.g. voluntary time, free use of equipment, premises ■ capital items, e.g. items to claim for on insurance ■ any other costs, e.g. entrance frees to museums, galleries

Source: ContinYou (2005a) *Fundraising Guidance. Study Support/Out-Of-School-Hours Learning (oshl).* Coventry: ContinYou.

Checklist for running a club as part of extended school activities

- ❑ **You are clear about what you want to achieve.**
- ❑ **You have assessed parental interest and likely demand in your plans.**
- ❑ **In planning the budget you have identified fund-raising needs, and how fees will be collected from children/ families.**
- ❑ **You have checked legislation and insurance requirements.**
- ❑ **You have determined premises and purchased essential materials, equipment and resources.**
- ❑ **You have recruited and appointed appropriate and sufficient staff and volunteers to support and run the club.**
- ❑ **You have set up a management committee (where appropriate).**
- ❑ **You have devised strategies for encouraging attendance of children and young people to the club.**
- ❑ **You have confirmed procedures for children registering on arrival and for their safety throughout the activity.**
- ❑ **You have prepared marketing and promotional information and distributed this in relevant locations.**
- ❑ **You have planned how best to evaluate the club outcomes.**
- ❑ **You have a clear idea of how you wish to further develop the club for the future.**
- ❑ **You have identified ways to give children greater responsibility and a say in how the club is run.**

Commercial activities in extended schools

The DfES, in partnership with the Consumer's Association and the Incorporated Society of British Advertisers (ISBA) have produced best-practice principles related to commercial activities undertaken in schools. These generic principles, which form a framework, are used to assess and develop a wide range of commercial activities targeted at schools which include:

- sponsored resources, e.g. teaching packs and materials;
- sponsored activities, e.g. competitions and projects;
- collector schemes, e.g. 'wrappers for books', computers for schools' supermarket vouchers.

The principles do not apply to activities such as exclusive licensing agreements, schools dedicated broadcasting or market research. The principles help teachers, parents and school governors to assess the commercial activity offered to the school which may form part of extended school activities, delivered by external partner providers. An extended school, which has established itself as a company, for example, may produce and sell their own teaching packs and materials to other schools.

The principles, set out in the form of a checklist below, will enable schools to judge the value of commercial activities delivered to them, or by them.

Table 3.3 Extended services/wrap-around care model review framework

	CHILDCARE	YOUTH SERVICES	OUT-OF-HOURS LEARNING	SPECIALIST SERVICES	SUPPORT FOR PARENTS	COMMUNITY USE
Where are we now?						
Where do we want to go?						
How will we get there?						
What do we have to do?						

Table 3.4 Model template of current and future extended school service provision 2007–10

School Name:____

2010 National target	Current extended services	Future extended services for 2010	Resources required	Partnerships/ Providers identified
1. VARIED MENU OF ACTIVITIES (OSHL) All schools to provide a varied menu of activities beyond school hours, which includes access throughout the week during term time and in some holidays. ■ Catch-up and stretch activities ■ Study support, homework clubs, breakfast clubs ■ Arts activities – dance, drama, media, music, arts and crafts ■ Sports activities (at least 2 hours per week) ■ Other recreational or specialist activities – ICT, foreign languages, volunteering, business and enterprise, environment and citizenship				
2a. CHILDCARE Schools to provide access to high-quality, affordable childcare, 8a.m. to 6p.m. all year (48 weeks), on site or through local registered providers or childminder networks, which meets national standards.				
2b. YOUTH ACTIVITIES All (secondary) schools open from 8a.m. to 6p.m., all year round, offering a range of activities for young people during term time and holidays. For example: music, sport and holiday activities. (Access to activities can be offered by the school itself on its premises or by another organisation on the school site or elsewhere nearby, at another school or at a sports centre).				

3. PARENTING SUPPORT INCLUDING FAMILY LEARNING All schools provide: ■ access to parenting groups/classes using structured, manual-based parenting programmes; ■ family learning sessions to allow children to learn with their parents; ■ information sessions for parents at phase transfer; ■ information about nationally and locally available sources of information, advice and support; ■ access to education, training and employment opportunities. ■ opportunities for parents to be involved in the life of the school, e.g. PTA, social events, volunteering (Access to activities can be offered by the school itself, or by signposting to other schools or third party providers in the voluntary, community, LA or private sectors).				
4. SWIFT AND EASY REFERRAL TO SPECIALISED SUPPORT SERVICES Pupils are able to obtain swift and easy access to specialist services from statutory and voluntary organisations, either on site or nearby the school. For example, education and social services, including services for children at risk, LAC, children with SEN/LDD; health services, including access to a school nurse, mental health services and other health services such as speech and language therapy.				
5. COMMUNITY ACCESS, INCLUDING ADULT LEARNING The school provides and promotes access to its premises and facilities for use by the wider community during the school day, evenings, weekends, school holidays. This includes: ■ access to a range of adult learning programmes; ■ access to ICT, sports or arts facilities. (Access to adult learning can be met through the school itself directly, by other schools or by facilities within their own cluster or local provider.)				

School checklist for assessing commercial activities

- ❑ Commercial activity adds educational value.
- ❑ The materials or activity do not encourage unhealthy, unsafe or unlawful activity for children.
- ❑ The business has clearly stated its purpose in producing the activity.
- ❑ The activity is based on accurate and current information.
- ❑ Any expressions of opinion are clearly distinguished from statements of fact.
- ❑ The activity is as free as possible of explicit sales messages.
- ❑ It has been made clear from the outset that the activity requires specialist resources.
- ❑ The commercial activity respects diversity of gender, race, disability and cultural issues reflected in contemporary UK society.
- ❑ The level of branding and logo use is appropriate to the activity.
- ❑ The activity or material has been developed with educators and piloted for school use with teachers and pupils, prior to production.
- ❑ The commercial activity or materials are relevant to the school and community context.
- ❑ The business or company has sought permission prior to forwarding the materials to the extended school.
- ❑ The sponsor and target audience for the activity/materials is clear.
- ❑ The school is able to engage in the activity free from unreasonable restrictions or conditions.
- ❑ The overall benefits of the collector scheme outweigh the costs to the school, pupils and parents.

Model extended school complaints policy

Maple School complaints policy against extended school provision

INTRODUCTION

This policy complements the school's general complaints policy, and has been drawn up by the governing body in consultation with the local authority. It meets the statutory requirements and procedures of the Education Act 2002 Section 29, and conforms to the DfES guidance on school complaints procedures (2003d).

This policy covers complaints about extended school activities and services provided **directly** by the school. Third-party providers of extended school provision have their own complaints policy and procedures. Any complaints about third-party external providers, services and activities must be sent to the head of the particular service or organisation, as well as to the headteacher of the school.

PRINCIPLES

- Parents and members of the community who have a complaint about extended activities and services provided directly by the school will have their complaint dealt with promptly, fairly, sensitively and effectively.
- The school complaints procedure will be transparent, respect confidentiality and be solution focused.
- All parties involved with the complaint will be kept informed of progress at all stages of the procedure.
- Realistic time limits for action will be made explicit to all parties and will be adhered to.

The five-stage complaints procedure

Stages 1, 2 and 3 are school-based and deal with complaints about extended school provision in partnership with complainants.

Stages 4 and 5 are formal and involve external bodies, i.e. the local authority and the Local Government Ombudsman or the Secretary of State for Education.

Stages 4 and 5 are only triggered in exceptional circumstances, after Stages 1 to 3 have been followed.

The following flow chart summarises the procedure.

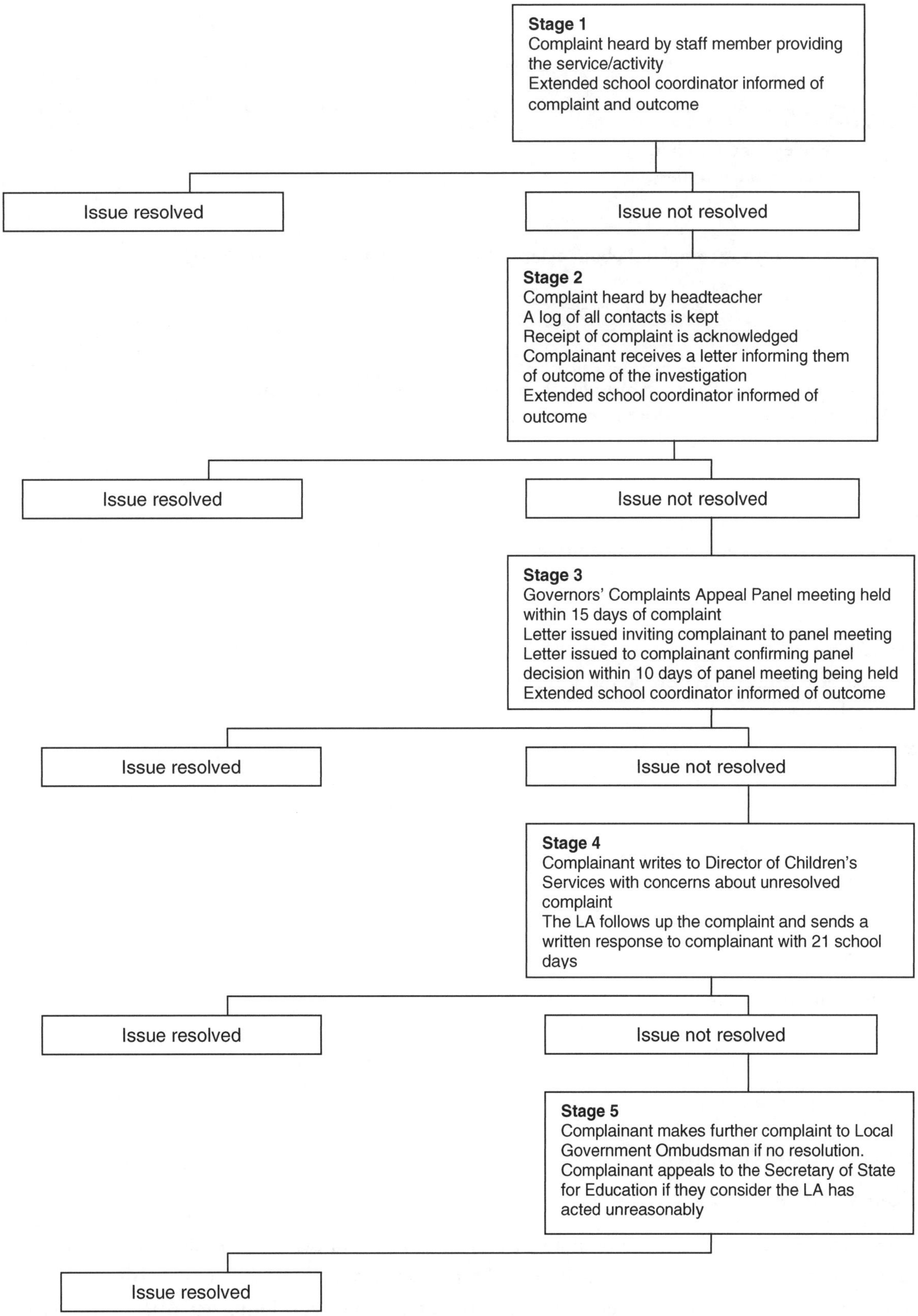

Figure 3.3 Summary of extended school complaints procedure

Table 3.5 Example of a complaint form. (Adapted from DfES 2003d)

Please complete this form and return to ______________________the extended school co-ordinator, who will acknowledge receipt and explain what action will be taken.

Your (complainant's) name: ______________________________

Address:

Postcode:
Daytime telephone number:
Evening telephone number:
Email address:

Brief details of your complaint about extended provision delivered directly by school:

What action, if any, have you already taken to try to resolve the complaint?
(Who did you speak to and what was the response?)

What actions do you consider might resolve the problem at this stage?

Please attach any paperwork to this form as evidence of action already taken by you and the school.

Signature:

Date:

Official use

Date acknowledgement sent to complainant:

By whom:

Complaint referred to:

Date:

Legal requirements

Complaints procedures

The extended school governing body must publicise their complaints procedures to all service users in relation to the activities, facilities and services provided by the school. Further information at: www.governornet.co.uk All third party providers offering activities and services through the school premises or using school facilities must have their own complaints procedures in place.

Charitable status

Foundation and voluntary schools are already corporate bodies with charitable status. The benefits of being a charity include tax concessions and exemptions, in some circumstances special treatment on VAT, and to be able to raise funds from the public, business and grant making trusts. Foundation and voluntary schools must seek advice about their proposals for extended school activities from the Charity Commission, the Inland Revenue and the Commissioner for Customs and Excise, as there are some restrictions. These schools must check the trust deed under which they have been established, to ensure that any proposed extended school activity falls within their charitable purposes. It may be necessary in some instances to make a formal application to the Secretary of State for the trust deed to be amended, for this purpose.

Further information about charitable status can be found on the following websites:

www.charity-commission.gov.uk
www.inlandrevenue.gov.uk/charities/index.htm

School companies

Sections 11 and 12 of the Education Act 2002 gives maintained schools the power to establish school companies on their own or with others (schools, LA) for specified purposes, i.e. to offer and run some extended services. The LA acts as a supervising authority to the school company. A school company can be a company limited by guarantee, i.e. a non-profit distributing organisation where any profits generated by the company are applied back into the furtherance of the organisation's objectives. Alternatively, a school can be a company limited by shares, i.e. any profit made is distributed back to members.

A school company must produce a Memorandum and Articles of Association. The Memorandum of Association sets out the company objectives and the powers it has to fulfil its objectives. The Articles of Association are the provisions which set out how the company will run on a practical level, e.g. composition of the board, membership and meeting requirements. An example of the membership of a school company includes: an independent chair, the headteacher, the deputy headteacher, a finance director, a company secretary, four community representatives, a LA representative and a member nominated by the PTA. The board meets five times a year and the minutes are open to scrutiny by governors.

Further information about this aspect of a school company can be found in Annex A of the DfES publication (2005k) entitled *Guidance on School Companies*, which can be downloaded from the following website: www.teachernet.gov.uk/management/atoz/s/schoolcompanies

The ContinYou/DfES leaflet (2005f) entitled *School Companies* is available from: www.teachernet.gov.uk/wholeschool/extendedschools/practicalknowhow

The School Company Regulations 2002 (SI No. 2978) is available from: www.hmso.gov.uk

It is wise to seek legal advice from a solicitor in relation to company structure. Forty per cent of directors of school companies must be non-executive, i.e. not employed by or contracted to the company to provide services. Directors must also be police checked. Other schools can be members of a school company. Governors of a school may serve as directors of the new company. However, the company is an independent entity in its own right.

School companies formed to purchase goods and services for their members will be acting as agents of the LA, and therefore the LA can reclaim any VAT incurred. Service delivery companies however will not be acting as agents of the LA because they will be spending income from the fees paid for provision (normal trading). A school can withdraw from a school company if 12 weeks' notice in writing is given to the company.

Schools who wish to become a company can achieve charitable status, but in such an instance the school company has to be independent of a third party, which includes a school or governing body.

It is more usual for a school to form a company limited by guarantee. The company will need its own bank account and accountants. The school company can provide goods, services and/or facilities to other schools for out-of-school-hours activities, e.g. play equipment, food for breakfast clubs and holiday play schemes.

Public entertainment and other licences

There are some extended school activities and services that require licences, e.g. community social events where alcohol is likely to be served on the school premises, and where concerts, films and performances are held on the school premises, an entertainment, theatre or cinema licence is required. Further advice and guidance about licences can be obtained from the LA.

Transfer of Control Agreements

Before the governing body of an extended school enters into a Transfer of Control Agreement it must obtain the LA's consent. This type of agreement relates to transferring control of the premises to another body during school hours, or sharing control of the school premises with another body (known as the 'controlling body'). The controlling body will control the occupation and use of the premises during the times specified in the agreement.

Transferring control of the premises to local community groups, sports associations and service providers enables school facilities to be used without needing ongoing management or administrative time from school staff.

The Agreement should include arrangements under which the governing body can regain control of the premises. Checking that there are no conflicts between the use to which premises may be put under the Transfer of Control Agreement and any trust deed for the school is important. Further information and a model Transfer of Control Agreement can be found at: www.teachernet.gov.uk/wholeschool/extendedschools/practicalknowhow

Letting premises for use by third-party providers

Where a trust deed or a Transfer of Control Agreement is not in place, it is the school's governing body that controls the use of the school premises during and outside school hours. In such instances it is good practice to provide third parties with the school's policy on the use of premises, i.e. protocols for using shared communal space, access, health and safety.

It is good practice to have a booking form for out-of-school-hours activities, which sets out the terms and conditions for use of premises and facilities, and acts as a legally binding agreement. Usage of premises falls into two main categories:

1. **unattended lettings** – where defined staff, e.g. site manager, or responsible adult, do not have to be present all the time, but open and close the premises,
2. **attended lettings** – where defined staff have to be present all the time.

It is not always a requirement for the school's site manager or headteacher to lock and unlock the school premises. This task can be delegated to other responsible adults nominated by the headteacher and approved by the governors.

Further information about letting of school premises can be found at: www.teachernet.gov.uk/schoolslandandproperty

Contracts for staff

A review of contractual obligations for existing staff may have to take place if they wish to become involved in extended school programmes. This needs to be done in conjunction with the body that employs them; usually the LA for staff who work at community and voluntary-controlled schools, or the governing body for staff working at a foundation or voluntary-aided school.

Insurance

The cost of school property insurance is not significantly affected by the wider community use of a school's premises out of school hours. However, it is wise to check this out with the LA risk manager and the school's insurance company. All schools are required to have public liability insurance and the governing body is responsible for insurance cover.

The school must check that any organisations, groups and providers have their own public liability insurance should any claims arise from their own activities. Some groups and providers with national affiliations may be covered by the organisation's overall insurance policy, but this needs checking. Further information on insurance for schools is available at: www.dfes.gov.uk/a-z/INSURANCE.html and www.dfes.gov.uk/valueformoney/

Data protection, information sharing and confidentiality

Schools must give consideration to whether offering extended school services could result in any additional issues relating to personal data, information or confidentiality. For example, health and social care service providers on the school site may possess confidential information. It is therefore important that the school checks that these specialist service providers adhere to individual professional guidelines.

Under the Data Protection Act 1998 certain information is exempt from disclosure and should be shared with other service providers. This includes:

- material whose disclosure would be likely to cause serious harm to the physical or mental health or emotional condition of the pupils or someone else;
- information about whether the child is or has been subjected to or may be at risk of suspected child abuse;
- references about pupils supplied to potential employers, to student admissions bodies, another school, a higher education/further education (HE/FE) institution, or any other place of education or training;
- information that may form part of a court report.

Further information about data protection can be found at: www.dfes.gov.uk/a-z and www.dataprotection.gov.uk

Confidentiality and information sharing guidance

- **Information sharing that respects confidentiality is a key principle, providing the welfare and safety of the child or young person is not 'at risk' or likely to be compromised.**
- **Each service provider and the school must make explicit their policy and requirements regarding confidentiality.**
- **The Data Protection Act, information sharing protocols and procedures are clear to all partners and are correctly followed.**
- **Any highly case sensitive information is password protected, and can only be accessed by authorised personnel, who are CRB checked.**
- **An initial 'Need to Know' policy is in operation, which answers five key questions:**
  - **What essential information is required?**
  - **Under what circumstances can this information be released?**
  - **To whom is it appropriate to release the information?**
  - **How will the information be used?**
  - **Will the released information be crucial to improving outcomes for the child?**
- **It is made explicit when written consent is required for the release of information.**
- **All confidential conversations about children and families take place in a private sound-proofed office.**
- **All staff know about the information sharing index: its purpose, information held and who can access information.**

Further information, and a helpful checklist in relation to information sharing protocols, can be found in the DfES document entitled: *Inter-Agency Information Sharing Criteria*, which is available and can be downloaded from the *Every Child Matters* website: www.everychildmatters.gov.uk

The following two documents, also available on the same website, will be helpful, in writing an extended school information sharing protocol:

> *A Framework for Information Sharing*, with a useful flow chart in Appendix 3 on, 'Do I need an operational information sharing agreement?' And, *A Step-by-Step Guide to Writing Information Sharing Protocols*.

Practicalities

Before an increased range of additional extended school activities and services are offered by the school, a review of some practical management aspects will be necessary. For example, the school may need to develop:

- more flexible opening hours;
- new visitor and school security procedures;
- revisions to health and safety policies;
- multi-agency staffing arrangements.

Staffing

Many extended school services and activities will be delivered by partners using their specialist knowledge, skills and expertise. Some existing school staff may be able to offer support in the planning and delivery of extended school activities but this is voluntary and optional.

Where schools utilise their own staff in extended school provision they can provide time off in lieu or make supplementary payments. Alternatively, community activities can become part of some school staff's core work with salary apportioned between budgets.

Some activities can be supported by parent or community volunteers, the school may consider payment of expenses in such instances. Any staff or providers delivering services to children and young people must be Criminal Records Bureau (CRB) checked.

Older school pupils, such as sixth formers, can be involved in supporting some extended school activities, but they must be overseen by a member of staff.

Information on procedures for employing staff is available at: www.dfes.gov.uk/a-z

CROSS-SERVICE/EXTENDED SCHOOL TRAINING PROGRAMME

This training programme has been planned and developed in partnership with staff from the school and multi-agencies, private providers.

The aspects included on the training programme have been jointly identified and agreed by participants. The ongoing training programme will be delivered in a flexible, personalised and blended learning environment.

This programme supports all those staff from within and outside school who provide extended services and activities.

Participants will be requested to complete an end-of-programme evaluation.

TRAINING PROGRAMME CONTENTS

- ❑ **Roles and responsibilities in extended schools** – partnerships, teamwork, networking, case study scenarios
- ❑ **Operational procedures** – record keeping, tracking progress
- ❑ ***Every Child Matters*** – principles, five outcomes
- ❑ **Inclusion** – policy, ethos, principles, accessibility to services, personalisation
- ❑ **Common Assessment Framework** – information sharing, confidentiality
- ❑ **National Service Framework** – implications for service delivery
- ❑ **Safeguarding children** – guidance and procedures
- ❑ **Health and safety** – procedures, policy, risk assessment
- ❑ **First aid**
- ❑ **Customer care** – service delivery, public liability
- ❑ **Quality assurance** – monitoring and evaluating service impact/outcomes
- ❑ **Using and analysing data**
- ❑ **Using ICT** – including multi-media technology
- ❑ **Dealing with the unexpected** – customer complaints, aggressive clients

Training

Providing extra training opportunities for staff, service providers and volunteers involved in extended school service delivery is useful for ensuring the quality of the programmes and customer care.

Child protection and safeguarding

Many extended school activities and services provide increased levels of access for adults to school premises. Where adults and children are jointly involved in activities, schools must ensure that there are always adequate staffing arrangements in place, so that children are not left unsupervised.

Standard school staff vetting procedures with the CRB need to be carried out if normal duties in extended school provision include regularly caring for, training, supervising or being in sole charge of children under 18 years of age, or vulnerable adults.

Further information about procedures for vetting staff can be found at: www.crb.gov.uk

Health and safety

The employer is responsible for the health and safety of their employees and non-employees who are on the school premises, under the Health and Safety at Work Act 1974 and associated regulations. Any external provider of a service must be familiar with and follow the procedures set out in the school's health and safety policy, which should be kept under regular review.

Risk assessments must be undertaken in relation to the provision of extended services and activities. Such an assessment considers the likely risks to staff, pupils, visitors and users of the premises.

Anyone providing extended school provision should be made aware of first aid arrangements in the school, particularly when out-of-school-hours activities are taking place.

Further detailed information on health and safety is available in the DfES publication entitled: *Health and Safety: Responsibilities and Powers*, which can be downloaded at:
www.teachernet.gov.uk/responsibilities and
www.dfes.gov.uk/a-z/HEALTH_AND_SAFETY.html

Safe Keeping: A Good Practice Guide for Health and Safety in Study Support is available from DfES publications (reference: DfEE 0197/2000).

Guidance on First Aid for Schools: A Good Practice Guide is available from teachernet website: www.teachernet.gov.uk/firstaid

Advice on risk assessment can be found on the DfES website:
www.dfes.gov.uk/a-z/RISK_ASSESSMENT.html

There is also a useful publication entitled *Five Steps to Risk Assessment* and details can be found at: http://213.212.77.20/pubns/raindex.htm

Accessibility

Under the Disability Discrimination Act 1995, the Special Educational Needs (SEN) and Disability Act 2001 and the Disability and Discrimination Act 2005, schools offering extended school provision must not treat disabled children, young people or adults less favourably. They must also make reasonable adjustments to ensure the disabled person is not put at a substantial disadvantage. By law schools must improve their accessibility arrangements in order to:

- improve access to goods and services;
- improve access to the physical environment which includes school premises;
- increase curriculum and out-of-school-hours learning access;
- improve access to written information by using alternative formats.

The extended school co-ordinator should collect and analyse data in order to identify how many disabled children, young people and adults are accessing extended school provision. This evidence will also enable future planning for extended school services to take account of the needs of disabled people. Further information about disabled access can be found on the Disability Rights Commission website: www.drc-gb-org

Net capacity and community space

The Net Capacity Assessment Method measures the numbers of pupil places available in schools. LAs can designate parts of a school's premises for community use, thereby excluding them from the school's net capacity. For example, school spaces may be excluded from the net capacity if they are used for early years and childcare or for adult learning and skills, or if they are specially resourced community facilities such as a youth centre or library. Small rooms such as community offices or stores are to be included in the net capacity assessment, but do not count towards the net capacity of the school. The Net Capacity Method does not apply to City Technology Colleges, City Academies, nursery schools, special schools or pupil referral units.

Further information on how school capacity is measured is available in the DfES publication entitled: *Assessing the Net Capacity of Schools*, which can be downloaded from: www.dfes.gov.uk/netcapacity

Planning permission

Planning permission will be required if there is any material change of use of land resulting from extended school services and activities. The governing body of the school must seek advice from the LA planning department.

If a school wishes to dispose of or change the use of its school playing fields, prior consent will need to be sought from the Secretary of State. The DfES Schools Assets Team can provide further information; it can be contacted by email at: assets.schools@dfes.gsi.gov.uk

Further information about school playing fields is available from: www.teachernet.gov.uk/schoolplayingfield

Advice on community use is available in: *Building Bulletin 95, Schools for the Future: Designs for Learning Communities*, available at: www.teachernet.gov.uk/schoolbuildings

School security

A review of school security should be undertaken in order to identify any possible additional risks by offering extended school activities and services. Ideally, security is easier to manage if areas used for out-of-school-hours and community activities are separate from the main school areas, which can be locked and secured separately.

Additional security lighting may be required if areas are used outside daylight hours. Responsible key holders must ensure areas are locked up and secure after evening, weekend or holiday use.

Schools should consult their LA if they wish to modify security arrangements due to increased community use.

Further information on school security is available at: www.teachernet.gov.uk/wholeschool/healthandsafety/schoolsecurity/guidance

School Security – Dealing with Troublemakers;
Can You See What They See?
A Legal Toolkit for Schools: Tackling Abuse, Threats and Violence towards Members of the School Community.

Managing School Facilities 4: Improving Security in Schools is available at: www.teachernet.gov.uk/sbpublicationsandguidance

Fire safety

When setting up and running extended school provision, the following fire safety procedures must be followed:

- ensure the necessary fire escape routes are open and accessible when only parts of the school are open for evening or weekend use;

- ensure fire exits are clearly signposted;
- fire drill procedures should be known by the providers of services;
- any equipment brought into the school for extended school activities by external providers must be checked for safety and be compatible with the school's electrical services;
- escape routes should have emergency lighting where any public performances are taking place on the school premises;
- conditions on the number of people present, the type of layout for seating, emergency lighting and the marking of emergency exits must be observed when members of the community are attending stage or film presentations on school premises.

Further information on general fire safety is included in *Managing School Facilities Guide 6*, available at: www.teachernet.gov.uk/fire

Buildings, facilities and maintenance

Some schools may need to provide additional facilities such as toilets, changing rooms and refreshment facilities, in order to prevent members of the public attending extended school activities and services having to go through school areas during the day.

Additional furniture, storage facilities and a reception area may also be required as a result of the expansion of extended school provision. Premises should be safe and fit for purpose for extended school provision. The governing body has control over the premises.

Maintenance and repairs of school premises and facilities will need to be more flexible, particularly when some extended school activities take place at the weekend or during the school holidays.

Maintenance activities such as cleaning and repairs should not disrupt the core activities of the school, during the day. Maintenance costs should be taken into account when setting charging rates for extended school services and activities.

Transport

When planning extended school provision, particularly those activities occurring at the weekends or outside the normal school day, some consideration needs to be given to how users are likely to travel to attend such activities. Not all families have their own car, and where possible, particularly in rural areas, extended school activities should coincide and fit in with public transport timetables. Schools in these areas may consider applying for a Vital Village grant or seek advice from their Rural Transport Partnership Office.

School car parks should be well lit and provide disabled parking. There should also be provision made for bicycle storage. Signs should be displayed to indicate that the school cannot be held responsible for any bicycles or vehicles left unattended and parked on the school site.

Further information relating to transport issues and extended school provision can be found at:

www.local-transport.dft.gov.uk/schooltravel
www.saferoutestoschools.org.uk
www.countryside.gov.uk/vitalvillages

The information in this chapter was taken from two DfES publications which can be downloaded from: www.teachernet.gov.uk/extendedschools

Extended Schools Providing Opportunities and Services for All (2002)
Extended Schools: Access to Opportunities and Services for All (2005)

The know-how series of ContinYou/DfES leaflets can be downloaded from: www.teachernet.gov.uk/wholeschool/extendedschools/practicalknowhow

Further activities for school leaders and heads of children's centres

The following questions are designed to enable you to discuss and identify positive ways forward in meeting the challenges posed by setting up and running extended school provision.

- How good are the local public transport links for aligning with out-of-school-hours activities?
- How accessible are your school premises and facilities for disabled members of the community?
- How safe are external school areas such as footpaths and car parks at night?
- Have you got contingency cover in place if the headteacher and site manager are not available to lock up school premises?
- Is there sufficient administrative capacity to cope with extended school clients registering for activities or enquiring about activities available?
- What potential exists to further develop the extended school's entrepreneurial capacity without compromising the core function of teaching and learning?
- What funding streams exist that can be used to support the development of extended services?
- How can you capitalise on any existing resources and relationships in order to obtain further funding?

4

How to Establish and Operate Effective Multi-agency Working and Community Engagement

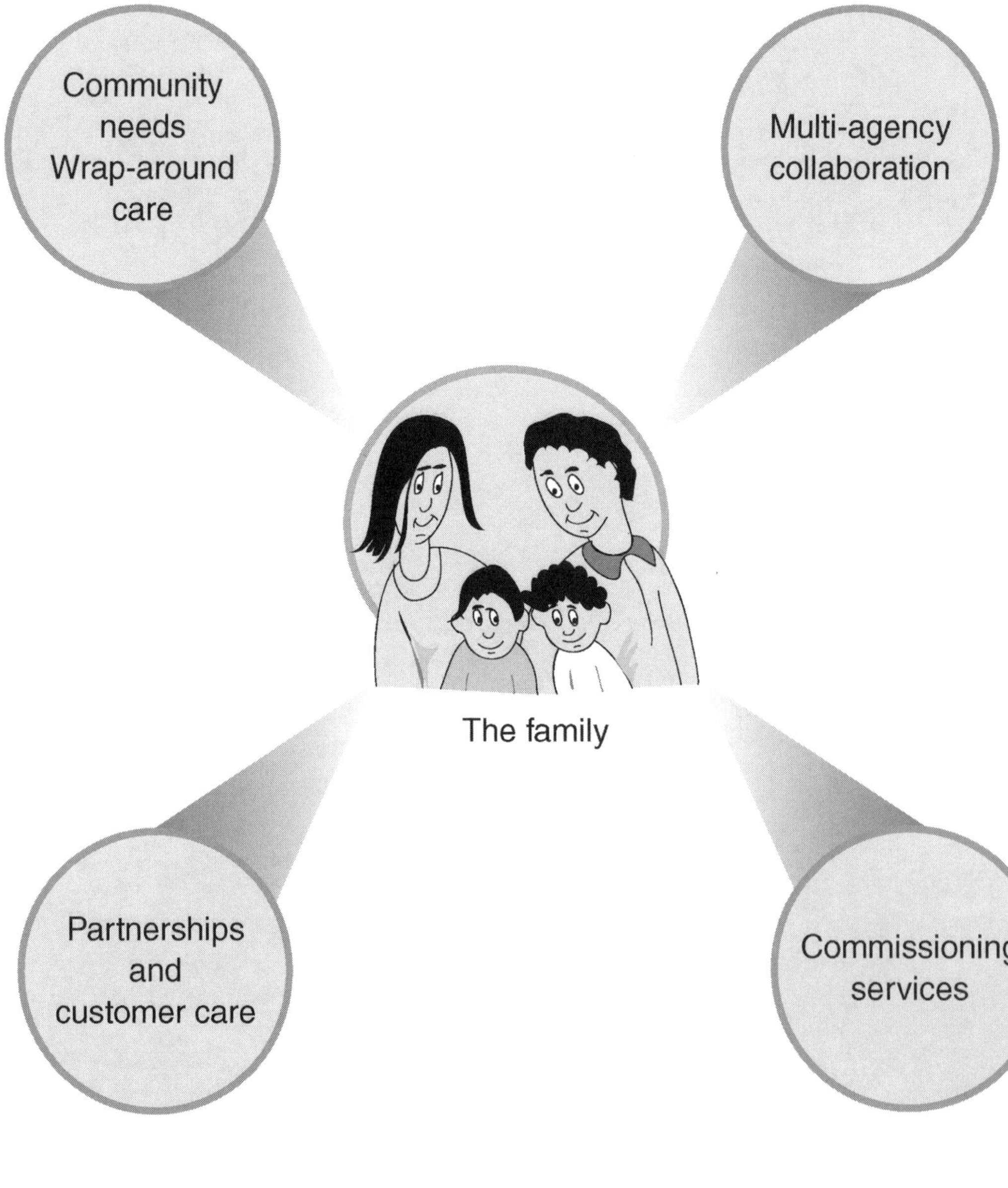

Principles and practice of effective multi-agency service provision

Special schools have been working collaboratively in partnership with multi-agency frontline workers for many years, providing wrap-around care, to meet the needs of the whole child. Several special schools already have multi-agency teams of health and social care professionals based on their site, offering inreach and outreach provision. There are lessons to be learnt from such schools in establishing similar provision in children's centres and full service extended schools.

The strategies and approaches recommended in this chapter are based on real examples of best practice already existing in the special sector and in co-located mainstream and special schools.

School leaders and heads of children's centres find this aspect of their work the most complex to develop. One headteacher commented:

> implementing the ECM agenda – in particular the multi-agency and community aspects – is hard work; it takes time and you can expect to run into problems along the way but when it works, it is amazing
>
> (NCSL 2006a: 26)

Different agencies have a tendency to work at different speeds. For example, education is used to working at a rapid pace, whereas health services take more time working with clients. While there is no blueprint for effective multi-agency working, or for overcoming the huge variations that exist in the way different services work, there are some key principles to follow. Table 4.1 provides a useful checklist for ensuring multi-agency partnership working runs as smoothly as possible within a children's centre or in a mainstream extended school.

Table 4.1 Key principles for effective multi-agency partnership working

Principle	Best practice examples
▪ Develop a common shared and agreed partnership principle and moral purpose based on ECM outcomes.	▪ The school or centre's mission statement, which reflects ECM outcomes, appears in all the multi-agency leaflets for service users and school/centre staff. ▪ The mission statement is displayed in the multi-professional well-being team base. ▪ A visioning event for all multi-agency, private, voluntary and community service providers working with the school/centre is held, which clarifies each other's aspirations and expectations for collaborative coherent partnership working.
▪ Common language/terminology is clarified and used between the school, centre and other multi-agency service providers.	▪ School/centre staff and all service providers have a glossary of terms related to ECM and wrap-around care, that provides a regular common point of reference.
▪ Roles and responsibilities of school, centre and multi-agency external service providers are made explicit, and are based on relationships of trust, mutual respect and team work.	▪ The first whole school/centre INSET day of the autumn term provides a session delivered by a range of frontline multi-agency workers who outline their respective roles, indicating how they complement the role of school/centre staff.

Table 4.1 *(Continued)*

Principle	Best practice examples
	■ A multi-agency brochure is provided to all school/centre staff, and vice versa, outlining and clarifying roles. ■ School/centre staff have a target set as part of the performance management or appraisal review process, which is specifically related to developing and contributing to collaborative partnership working with multi-agency professionals.
■ Realistic agreed cross-service/school or children's centre targets and priorities are set for the delivery of wrap-around care and extended school service provision.	■ A summary of the school/centre service delivery development plan priorities and activities is incorporated into the staff handbooks for multi-agency workers and school/centre staff. ■ All services delivered make reference to these priorities and activities in their planning, and also in their evaluation of impact and outcomes of service provision.
■ The profile of the multi-agency team is raised in whole school/children's centre.	■ ECM achievement of the month celebrations take place at staff briefings, which reflect school/centre and multi-agency successful team working. ■ Work shadowing activities take place. ■ Joint action research projects and initiatives take place which reflect successful collaborative partnership work. ■ Trainees from health and social care undertake work placements within the school or children's centre setting.
■ A dedicated central base is provided for the multi-agency team, located near the staffroom.	■ The base is clearly signposted. ■ The range of programmes and services offered and 'drop-in' information sessions are publicised, along with opening and closing times. ■ Dedicated administrative support is provided for the multi-agency team. ■ Multi-agency staff have full access to and are welcomed into the staffroom.
■ There is an annual cross-service/school or children's centre CPD programme available which supports the ECM agenda.	■ Joint training activities are a regular feature, delivered in a range of flexible ways, e.g. distance learning via CD-ROM, e-conferencing, coaching and mentoring, direct taught sessions.
■ New multi-agency, external service delivery partners or teaching and support staff joining the setting receive a comprehensive induction programme within the school or children's centre.	■ Each new member of internal or external staff is paired up with a staff buddy from the school or centre. ■ There is a comprehensive ECM induction handbook provided. ■ Joint induction specific training takes place. ■ Cross-team/school/centre induction meetings are held.

Table 4.1 *(Continued)*

Principle	Best practice examples
■ Weekly operational multi-agency/external service provider meetings are held on site.	■ Meetings are led by the deputy head, or head of children's centre. The extended school co-ordinator and SENCO are in attendance. ■ Meetings share concerns, good practice and report on progress/outcomes.
■ Monthly multi-agency professional strategic meetings take place on site.	■ These meetings are developmental, solution focused and are comprised of line managers, team leaders of multi-agency frontline workers and the headteacher and deputy headteacher/centre head.
■ Multi-agency workers and other external service providers/partners are invited to contribute to planning and decision making about future provision.	■ Representatives from multi-agency, voluntary, community and independent service providers are on the management board, the governing body and/or focus groups of the extended school/centre. ■ External providers and staff from multi-agencies complete an annual survey.
■ Multi-agency workers engage clients in the review of their own well-being progress and service provision to inform future programmes.	■ Parents/carers, children, young people complete a survey or contribute verbal comments during reviews of progress and provision. This is fed back into the school/children's centre self-evaluation process.
■ Multi-agency frontline workers are line managed by their service manager/team leader.	■ The head of children's centre or deputy headteacher support the work of these professionals by providing a link between school and multi-agency staff in partnership with the extended school co-ordinator and SENCO/INCO.
■ Inreach and some outreach work occurs with other local schools and families in the community.	■ Outreach work is commissioned and does not compromise inreach work or the quality of the multi-agency well-being team. ■ Service level agreements operate for outreach and inreach work.

The approach school leaders and heads of children's centres need to adopt in developing effective multi-agency partnership working is one that identifies and clarifies with each other how the school and each respective agency or service provider achieve their aims. This protocol approach reduces any suspicion that might arise between agencies, the school and individuals.

Developing protocols between schools and services

The need for a protocol arises when two organisations/services begin to work more closely together. The development of a protocol results in greater clarity to service delivery. The aim and purpose of any protocol is to acknowledge and enhance positive relationships between the parties.

The function of a protocol

A protocol:

- **helps the school and service to develop a common language and understanding of how their different organisational cultures operate;**
- **makes explicit the expectations of both the agency and the school as to their respective roles and responsibilities in the provision and receipt of services;**
- **provides a systematic approach from initial referral to case closure;**
- **provides clarity and direction in the midst of change within schools and services;**
- **provides a clear grievance process where a relationship between a school and service encounters difficulties.**

A protocol cannot account for any inadequacies in the overall service systems, i.e. the lack of services.

Guidance for devising a written protocol

The following guidance will enable headteachers, heads of children's centres and heads of service, including front-line service workers, to know what essential and important information to include in each section of the protocol, when drawing this up together.

1. Parties to the protocol

The parties involved in the agreement and protocol, e.g. school and service.

2. Protocol background

Relevant information which provides a context for the protocol, e.g.

- a general description of the activities or services the parties will utilise and provide;
- the reason why the protocol is needed;
- the overall expectations of each organisation/service;
- other procedures and policies which impact on the protocol.

3. Scope and duration of the protocol

- Specify the areas of activity that the protocol covers, and what the protocol does not do.
- Specify the protocol period of operation, including the review date.

For example:

> *This protocol applies to all pupils referred from Maple School to Health, Social Care and Education Services. The protocol applies to agreed practices in relation to referral, case management, information sharing and informed consent. It also covers the roles and responsibilities of frontline workers from Health, Social Care and Education Services, when working in Maple School directly with pupils and/or parents, on the school site.*
>
> *This protocol does not override other existing protocols that the school and multi-agency services recognise and follow.*
>
> *This protocol will commence from the 1 September 2007. It will be reviewed on the 1 February 2008 and every year. The person(s) responsible for the review are:* ____________________

4. Aims of the protocol

This section identifies what all parties to the agreement are hoping to achieve through the development of the protocol. For example:

The aim of this protocol is to formalise the working relationship between Maple School and Health, Social Care and Education Services. In so doing, it clarifies the arrangements for the availability and provision of services to children and young people at Maple School from Health, Social Care and Education Services.

5. Description of services provided

A description of the activities and services that the protocol covers on the school site, and off-site, such as outreach or recreation inputs, from external services and providers should be briefly listed. For example:

- when and for how long the activities and services will be delivered, e.g. during or after the school day, for a period of 6–12 weeks;
- how the activities or services will be delivered, e.g. venue, time;
- who will deliver the activities or services;
- how information about the activities or services will be shared with parents/carers and school staff.

6. Target group

Include in this section information about:

- who is targeted by the service or activities to be provided;
- the eligibility criteria, e.g. age, gender, nature/severity of need;
- the additional needs, e.g. LDD (learning difficulties and disabilities), SEN, LAC (looked after children) of the target group;
- any other target groups who would benefit from such a service, e.g. parents/carers, school staff.

7. Referral/Case management practices

This section of the protocol must detail and clarify:

- the process for making and accepting referrals to the service, including how any waiting lists are managed;
- principles concerning informed consent;
- principles concerning information sharing, with whom, where and how;
- case management – who has responsibility for managing the case and monitoring the pupil(s);
- the process of case closure when a service is no longer required by a pupil and/or their family.

8. Legal responsibilities of each party

This section should include information about the duty of care to take reasonable action to avoid injury or harm to others, making legal responsibilities explicit for the school and the service(s). In addition to health and safety, it will also refer to any specific legislation relating to SEN and disability, equal opportunities, racial discrimination, safeguarding. Other issues to cover in this section include:

- transport and its related supervision in conveying children to and from off-site services and activities;
- obtaining parental permission – informed consent;
- dealing with statutory clients, e.g. LAC, statemented children.

9. Roles and responsibilities of each party to the protocol

Detail of the roles and responsibilities of each organisation/service that is party to the protocol needs to be outlined. For example, Maple School will:

- consult with the multi-agency worker before the service commences and negotiate and agree requirements;
- organise any resources and equipment needed for service delivery on the school site, e.g. a quiet room, a telephone, office or photocopier;
- check any school staff are made available when required to meet with front-line service workers to discuss pupil progress and follow-up.

The Service will:

- negotiate needs for service delivery on the school site;
- notify the school as soon as possible, if the front-line worker is unable to deliver the service, at any time;
- inform the school contact person if the service delivery is to take place in a different venue;
- attend case conference meetings at the school, as required;
- share relevant information about the pupil and the outcomes from service interventions, without breaching confidentiality, except where a client (child/young person) may be 'at risk';
- inform the school contact person when the service is completed for a pupil(s).

10. Resources to be supplied by each party

This section details the allocation of responsibility by each party for the provision of resources needed to deliver quality services. It also covers practical issues such as who covers direct and indirect costs. For example, external multi-agency services will provide:

- any specialist equipment, resources for service delivery;
- any written materials and information.

Maple School will provide:

- an appropriate room for service delivery, with telephone access;
- access to a meeting room;
- access to a photocopier;
- the loan of any audio visual equipment to deliver school training for staff, governors, parents/carers, pupils.

11. Monitoring and evaluation process

This section of the protocol details the process for monitoring and evaluating the activities and services provided. For example:

- What will be monitored and evaluated?
- How often will the service/activities be monitored and evaluated?
- What methods of monitoring and evaluation will be used?
- Who will contribute to the monitoring and evaluation process?
- How will findings from the evaluation be utilised and fed back?

12. Grievance procedures

This section outlines the steps to take if any difficulties arise while services are being delivered to the school. For example, where the school has a grievance:

Step 1: Discuss the issue with the front-line service worker concerned.
Step 2: Discuss the issue with the front-line service worker's line manager, if not resolved.
Step 3: If the grievance remains unresolved, then register it in writing, sending it to the front-line worker's line manager and to the team leader for the local service.
Step 4: If grievance still remains unresolved, write to the PCT manager, the Director of Social Services or the Director of Children's Services.
(Also refer to the model extended school complaints policy and procedure provided in Chapter 3.)

If the service has a grievance with the school:

Step 1: Discuss the issue with the member of school staff concerned.
Step 2: If necessary, discuss the grievance with the Deputy Headteacher or whoever has responsibility for leading on pupil well-being in the school.
Step 3: If grievance remains unresolved, put this in writing and send to the Headteacher of the school and the Chair of Governors, who, on receipt of the letter, should convene a meeting to resolve the grievance.
Step 4: If the grievance still cannot be resolved, then put the grievance in writing and send to the Director of Children's Services, who will respond in writing to resolve the grievance.

13. Protocol review

The protocol should be reviewed formally every year. It is for the school and the service provider to agree a date and organise this review. It should be made explicit whose responsibility it is to update the protocol. In addition, it should make clear in this section how any new front-line service workers or new staff joining the school are made aware of the protocol.

14. Protocol signed

Both parties sign and date the written protocol and it is distributed to relevant personnel from the school and the respective service(s).

Table 4.2 Protocol framework for joint service/school partnership working

PROTOCOL TEMPLATE

1. Parties to the protocol

School/Service	Contact person	Position/Title	Contact details (phone, email)

2. Protocol background

3. Scope and duration of the protocol

4. Protocol aims

5. Description of services or activities to be provided

6. Target client group

7. Referral/Case management practices

8. **Legal responsibilities of each party**
9. **Roles and responsibilities of each party**
10. **Resources to be supplied by each party**
11. **Monitoring and evaluation processes**
12. **Grievance procedures**
13. **Protocol review**
14. **Protocol signed**

This is an agreement between Maple School and ______________________________ Service.

Signed: ______________________________ Date: ____/____/________
(Headteacher)

Signed: ______________________________ Date: ____/____/________
(Head of service/organisation)

Table 4.3 An introduction to Maple School Extended School Well-being Team

An introduction to Maple Extended School Well-being Team

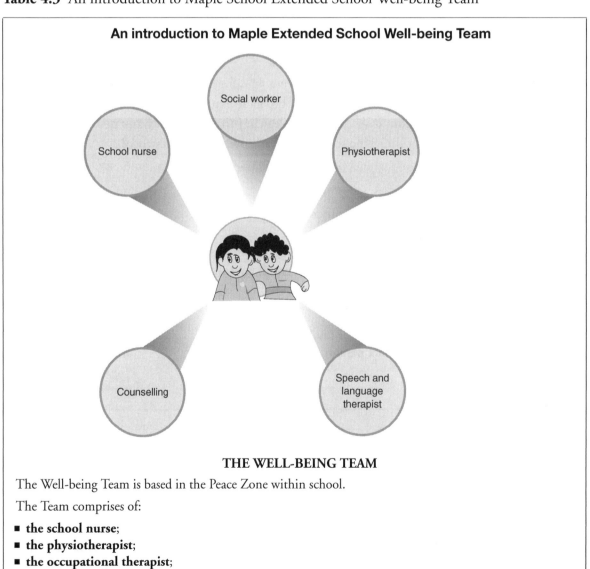

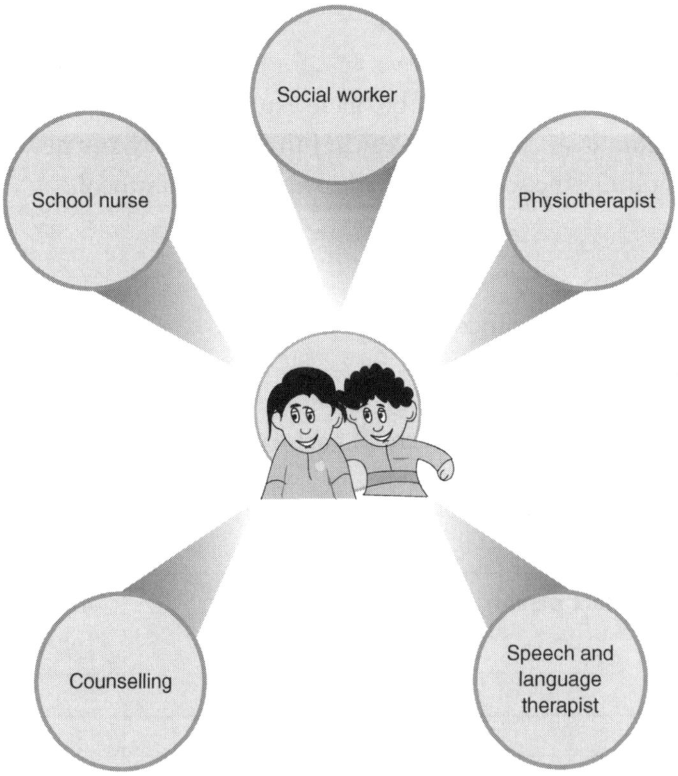

THE WELL-BEING TEAM

The Well-being Team is based in the Peace Zone within school.

The Team comprises of:

- **the school nurse;**
- **the physiotherapist;**
- **the occupational therapist;**
- **the speech and language therapist;**
- **the pupil counsellors;**

Table 4.3 *(Continued)*

- **the social worker**;
- **the alternative well-being therapist** – offering aromatherapy, relaxation techniques, head, hand and feet massage.

The Leader for Pupil Well-being (Deputy headteacher) oversees and supports the work of this team in school.

Referral of pupils to the team is made through the school's Co-ordinator for Additional Needs/SENCO, in consultation with parents/carers.

Pupils can self-refer and avail themselves of the 'drop-in' facilities offered by the School Nurse and the Pupil Counsellors.

The overall role of the Well-being Team is to remove and minimise barriers to learning caused by health problems. This ensures that pupils enjoy and achieve, and fulfil their optimum potential.

The role of the school nurse

- Assess, protect and promote the health and well-being of pupils.
- Offer advice, care and treatment to individual and groups of pupils, and their parents/carers.
- Act as a first point of contact to pupils and parents/carers who need health advice and information.
- Offer 'drop in' sessions to pupils and staff.
- Support pupils with ongoing specific health needs.
- Support, initiate and deliver activities to support PSHE and the Healthy Schools Programme.

The role of the physiotherapist

- Assess pupils' mobility and provide physiotherapy programme to meet needs, and or specialist aids, e.g. splint, standing frame.
- Improve pupils' mobility, posture, sitting balance, co-ordination, muscle strength, muscle flexibility, standing stability, walking skills.
- Monitor and evaluate pupils' progress throughout the programme.
- Provide advice, guidance and information to school staff and parents about back care, safe transfer and lifting techniques, correct use of hoists.
- Work with individual or small groups of pupils within school.
- Provide physiotherapy sessions to pupils from other local schools.
- Liaise with other health professionals where appropriate.

The role of the occupational therapist

- Assess pupils and plan an individual programme to improve their co-ordination, perception, sensation.
- To provide pupils who have physical limitations due to injury, illness, developmental delay with purposeful age-appropriate activities aimed at enabling them to participate in school life, self-care, play and leisure.
- Provide advice and guidance to parents/carers and school staff on activities to enhance and improve participation, as well as about classroom furniture, equipment adaptations.
- Monitor and evaluate pupil progress on the programme.
- Assist pupils to achieve maximum potential for functional independence, to gain maximum benefit from learning.

The role of the speech and language therapist

- Assess pupils' speech, language and communication needs.
- Provide programmes to support the development and improvement of speech, language and communication skills.
- Work with any pupils who have eating and swallowing problems, and offer advice on developing eating and drinking skills, working with the occupational therapist.
- Work closely with parents/carers, school staff to implement appropriate speech, language and communication programmes.
- Work with individual and groups of pupils within school.
- Provide advice and guidance to school staff on appropriate resources and activities to support the development of speech, language and communication skills, across the curriculum.
- Monitor and evaluate pupil progress on speech, language and communication programmes.

Table 4.3 *(Continued)*

The role of pupil counsellors

- Listen to pupils who share problems.
- Provide counselling to address specific issues, e.g. for bereavement, anxiety, behaviour, stress.
- Provide self-help practical strategies to enable the pupil to overcome and manage the problem.
- Contribute to any school-based training programmes, i.e. training peer counsellors.

The role of the social worker

- Act as a link between the school staff, the pupil and the family.
- Provide individual and small group support and counselling for pupils who have emotional, behavioural and social difficulties.
- Deliver workshops to strengthen parenting skills.
- Support pupils, parents and staff in the process of problem resolution.

The role of the alternative well-being therapist

- Provide a range of relaxation techniques to pupils, staff, parents/carers.
- Enable pupils, parents/carers, staff to cope with stress.
- Equip pupils, parents/carers, staff with strategies to manage their emotions.
- Create a sense of peace and calm for clients.

Further information

The school well-being team works largely with pupils who have more complex additional needs.

Further information about the well-being wrap-around care services offered in the Peace Zone can be found in the school's Parent Information Centre, which opens Monday to Friday from 8a.m. to 6p.m. and on Saturday morning from 10a.m. to 12 noon.

The school website also has information about the team and the services offered:
www.mapleextsch.co.uk/wellbeing

Table 4.4 Model extended school service agreement

Model extended school service agreement

Maple School welcomes your valuable contribution to its programme of extended school services. The aim of all extended school service provision is to meet the *Every Child Matters* outcomes. This agreement clarifies what to expect from Maple School, as the purchasing agency. The agreement also outlines what Maple School expects from you in the delivery of your service.

This agreement commences from (date, month, year) ________________ and was made by and between Maple School and (service provider) ________________________ and will end on (date, month, year) ____

This agreement may be renewed each year upon mutual agreement by both parties.
This agreement may be terminated at any time by either party.
In the event of termination, the provider will be paid for services already delivered, prior to termination of the agreement.

The agreed service being provided is: ____
No. of sessions/duration of the service: ______________________________________

In return for the service(s) delivered, Maple School agrees to:

- include you in the cross-service extended school training programme
- provide you with a copy of the extended school service handbook
- make you fully aware of the school's policies for customer care, equal opportunities, health and safety, and safeguarding
- keep you informed about any possible changes or developments to extended school provision
- provide you with a safe and healthy working environment

Table 4.4 *(Continued)*

- listen to any concerns you may have in relation to the delivery of your service
- welcome any feedback in relation to how the school can further improve the quality and delivery of its extended services.

I (Name of service provider) ______________________________ agree to:

- be CRB checked if not already covered for Enhanced disclosure
- deliver a good quality service that meets the needs of the client group
- provide evidence and feedback to the extended school co-ordinator on the attendance levels, client satisfaction, expenditure curtailed for materials, outcomes and impact of the service
- follow the school's policy and procedures for health and safety, safeguarding, equal opportunities, customer care, at all times, during service delivery
- provide the headteacher with written verification of public liability insurance, **prior** to this agreement being signed
- ensure that the room and any equipment used is left in good order after use
- accept full responsibility for any damage to, or loss of, school property during the delivery of my service
- provide advance warning in the event of being unable to deliver the service

Signed on behalf of (Name of service, charity, voluntary, independent or community organisation):

______________________________ Position: ______________________________

Signature: Name: (Print) ______________________________ Date: __________

Signature (of person directly delivering the service) ______________________________ Date: __________

Name (Print) ______________________________

There are three main multi-agency models in existence. These are outlined in Table 4.5.

Table 4.5 Models of multi-agency working

Multi-agency panel	**Multi-agency team**
■ Practitioners remain employed by their home service agency. ■ They meet regularly as a panel or network to discuss children with additional needs who would benefit from a multi-agency input. ■ Case work is sometimes carried out by panel members themselves, or in more strategic panels, by key workers assigned to lead on case work. ■ The Youth Inclusion and Support Panel (YISP) is an example of this model.	■ Practitioners from various agencies are seconded or recruited into the team. ■ The multi-agency team has a team leader. ■ The team works to a common purpose and common goals which are underpinned by the ECM outcomes. ■ Practitioners generally maintain links with their home service agency for supervision and training. ■ The team engage within universal service delivery at a range of levels, e.g. with individual children and young people, as well as with small group, family and school/centre work. ■ Behaviour and Education Support Team (BEST) and Youth Offending Team (YOT) are an example of this model.

Table 4.5 *(Continued)*

Integrated service
■ Several services share a common location, working together in a collaborative way. ■ They form a visible service hub for the local community. ■ The management structure facilitates integrated working. ■ There is a commitment by partner providers to find/facilitate integrated service delivery, e.g. pooled budgets. ■ Integrated services are delivered from a school or early years setting. ■ Examples of this model include Sure Start children's centres and full service extended schools.

Multi-agency planning to identify local problems and possibilities

Undertaking a Situation and Option Analysis can help multi-agency services, private, voluntary and community-sector providers, schools and children's centres to understand local issues and develop services and facilities that will help to resolve the issues.

The process is simple, and involves developing a 'Problem tree' which can be transformed into an 'Objectives tree'. The exercise is useful to repeat with different stakeholders, e.g. children, young people, parents/carers and members of the community.

A worked example of a problem tree transformed into an objectives tree, is illustrated below. Both are taken from the Centre for International Development and Training, University of Wolverhampton, Logical Framework Approach.

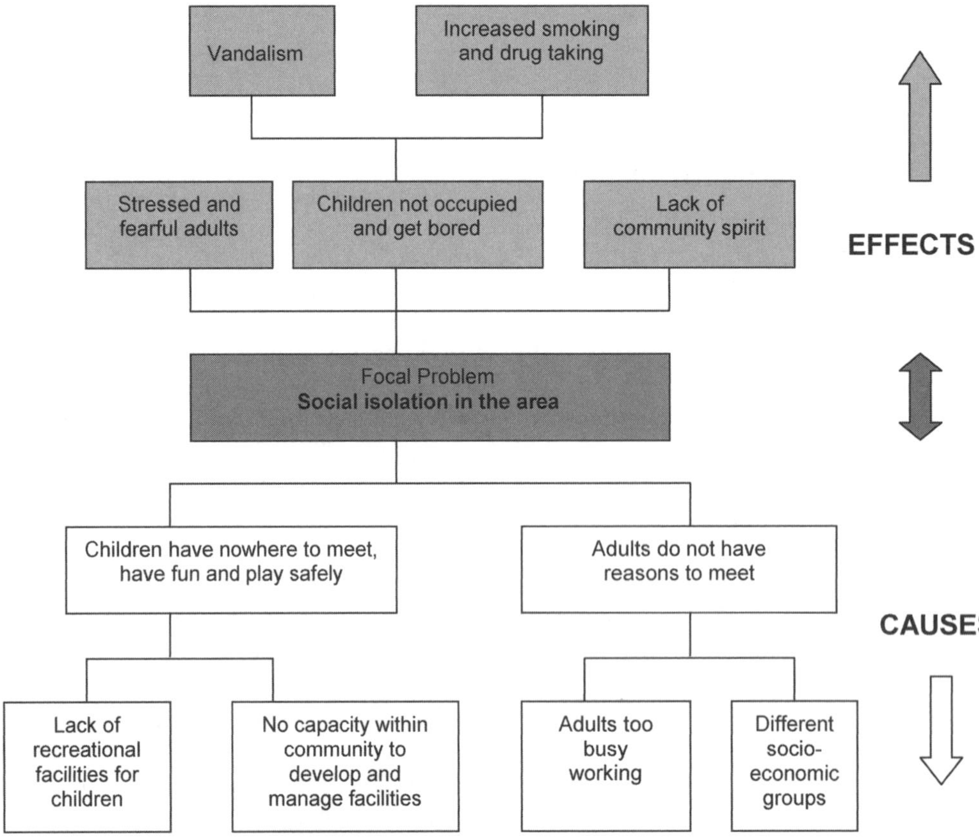

Figure 4.1 A problem tree example

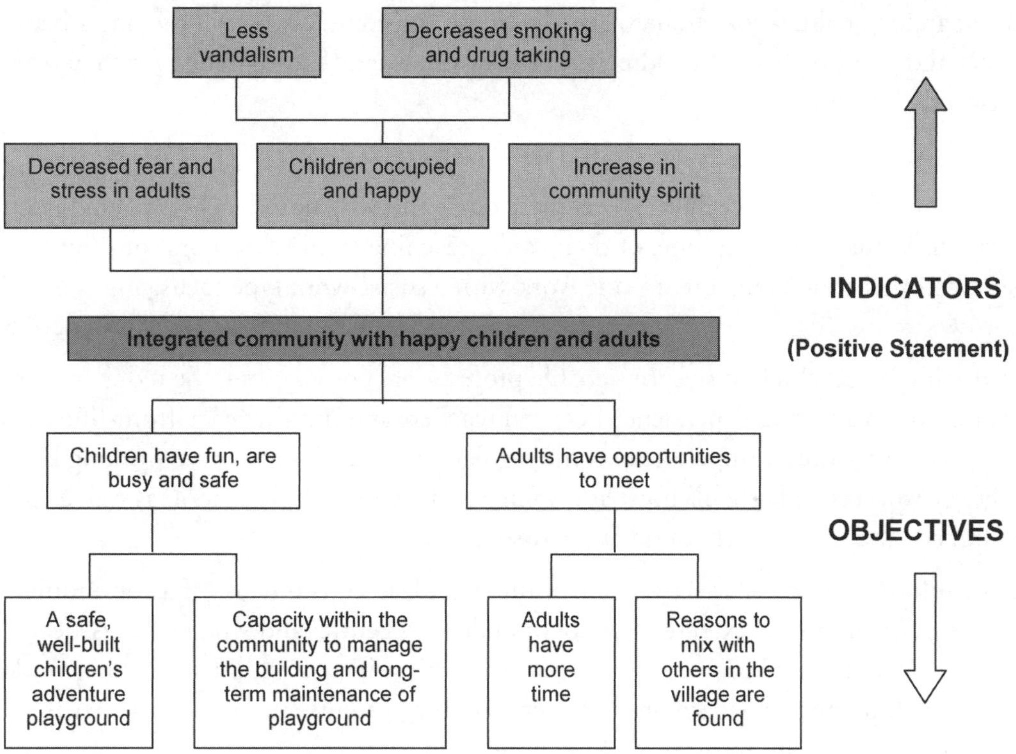

Figure 4.2 An objectives tree example

Partnerships crossing professional boundaries

Having a shared vision and trust are the essential prerequisites to producing effective collaborative partnership working, and for building coherence:

> Partnership needs to be worked at, it's about building on trust, it's about having the right people in the right place at the right time. . . .
>
> (DfES 2005b: 80)

The building of trust between multi-agency staff and those in educational settings takes time. This process, known as adaptive professionalism, is evident when teachers begin to understand, recognise and accept that professionals from other services can address pupils' well-being needs best, thus allowing them to focus on their core role of teaching for learning.

The draft revised professional standards for classroom teachers (April 2006), expect teachers to:

- recognise and respect the contribution that colleagues (*health and children's services professionals*) make to the development and well-being of children and young people;
- collaborate effectively with colleagues (*health and children's services professionals*) and work co-operatively in teams;
- know when to draw on the expertise of colleagues, such as those with responsibility for the safeguarding of children and young people and special educational needs, and to refer to sources of information, advice and support from external agencies.

Paul Ennals, Chief Executive of the National Children's Bureau and Chair of the Children's Workforce Network commented:

> An integrated qualifications framework, due to be agreed by 2010, will provide a better understanding of the role of children's services workers and greater scope for them to develop their skills.

He goes on to add:

> People are picking more flexible careers these days, and why not? Teachers could benefit enormously from spending some of their career teaching in the classroom, but then spending other time doing one-to-one work with a social-work type focus.
>
> (*Society Guardian* 2006: 2)

Extended schools and children's centres enable professional boundaries to be redrawn through the adoption of greater interdependence between teachers and multi-agency front-line workers, where mutual respect and team effort become regular practice. Collaborative working between multi-agency workers and schools must add value to the efforts of the school, as well as provide services outside the realm of school staff expertise.

Agencies work together most effectively when there is a lead co-ordinator or a community improvement partner in the extended school or children's centre; and when there is clear communication and agreed protocols for working practices in existence. Establishing working protocols and clear contractual arrangements ensures that parents and other users have confidence in and trust the agencies working with them.

Cross-sector working between health, education, social services and other agencies is most successful when those responsible for managing and developing extended services are well informed of the remit of different agencies and how the impact of their joint working is judged. Leaders of schools, children's centres and services as well as local authorities need to record and measure more systematically the impact of extended service provision on raising standards and improving the lives of children, young people and their families.

The most effective providers ensure that extended services are shaped and developed gradually, to reflect their community's needs and wants, in collaboration with other agencies.

Safer School Partnerships

Safer School Partnerships (SSPs) were launched in September 2002, based on a model from the United States. The aim of the scheme is to build good relationships of trust and mutual respect between the police, children and young people. SSP adopts a joined-up approach to crime prevention, school safety, behaviour improvement and educational achievement.

Safer School Partnerships integrate with the government's 'Respect' agenda, local area agreements, neighbourhood policing and extended schools.

The SSP approach takes different forms, dependent on the levels of funding available, the needs and views of the school and the local policing strategy for the community. Current approaches for SSP include:

- a fully operational police officer based full-time in a school working closely with a member of the school's senior management team, project worker and administrator;
- police officers seconded to Behaviour Education Support Teams (BESTs), and working with this multi-agency partnership in a secondary school and its feeder primary schools;
- police officers, both full-time and part-time, mainly providing reactive support to a cluster of schools in SSP style of policing;
- police officers or police community support officers (PCSOs) based with the neighbourhood policing team, working part-time in a problem-solving as well as an educational role.

To ensure an SSP is effective the following management procedures need to be in place:

- Establish a Strategic Steering Group to set the strategic direction and manage decision making.
- Establish a Management Steering Group to focus on the practicalities of managing the partnership on a day-to-day basis.
- Embed the work of SSP into the overall school behaviour policy.
- Have clear objectives, targets and mechanisms for measuring outcomes.
- Establish clear protocols between the police, school and other agencies.
- Work closely with Children's Trusts.
- Embrace youth participation – e.g. peer mediation as part of restorative justice, consult with young people and involve them in the design of activities and interventions aimed at reducing offending behaviour, truancy and exclusions.
- Ensure effective information sharing.
- Integrate SSP with neighbourhood policing.

Safer School Partnerships contribute to and support the achievement of the five *Every Child Matters* outcomes. Table 4.6 will assist headteachers in identifying how the SSP Quality Standards align with the *Every Child Matters* five outcomes as it makes the links between the two explicit.

Table 4.6 Links between *Every Child Matters* and SSP Quality Standards (Adapted from DfES 2006a)

ECM outcomes	**Safer School Partnerships Quality Standards**
Be healthy	■ promote healthy lifestyles ■ address drug and alcohol misuse ■ identify those at risk of offending, neglect or abuse
Stay safe	■ ensure staff are CRB checked and at least one is child-protection trained ■ comply with Health and Safety legislation ■ ensure child protection concerns are picked up and passed on as appropriate ■ promote anti-discriminatory behaviour and prevent bullying ■ reduce young people's experience of, and involvement in, crime and anti-social behaviour ■ steer young people away from involvement in criminal gangs
Enjoy and achieve	■ promote young people's attendance at school ■ ensure young people are in full-time education, training or employment ■ help young people make full and constructive use of their leisure time ■ provide positive and accessible recreational activities for young people
Make a positive contribution	■ ensure young people are fully involved in the design and development of Safer School Partnership activities ■ reduce the experience of bullying and anti-social behaviour (ASB) of young people in the Safer School Partnership's neighbourhood ■ provide opportunities for young people to contribute to the local community through active citizenship
Achieve economic well-being	■ promote the engagement of young people in education ■ assist in the preparation of the young person for further education, training and employment ■ ensure young people involved in Safer School Partnership are linked into further support where required

(Adapted from DfES 2006a: 24–5)

The DfES publication (2006a) *Safer School Partnerships – Mainstreaming* can be downloaded from the following website: www.everychildmatters.gov.uk/ete/ssp/

You can also email: sspmainstreaming@crimeconcern.org.uk

Other good sources of information can be found on the following websites:

www.saferschoolpartnerships.com
www.teachernet.gov.uk/wholeschool/behaviour/saferschoolpartnerships

Information about *Monitoring and Evaluating the Safer School Partnership Programme-Youth Justice Board 2005* can be found on the website: www.youth-justice-board.gov.uk/Publications

Details about neighbourhood policing can be obtained from the website: www.neighbourhoodpolicing.com

Further details about the *National Evaluation of the Restorative Justice in Schools Programme* can be found at the following website: www.youth-justice-board.gov.uk/Publications

Education Improvement Partnerships

Education Improvement Partnerships (EIPs) are designed to promote greater local collaboration across schools, usually in a geographical area, for school improvement and better service delivery. These can be between 5 and 30 schools in an EIP.

The main objectives of an EIP are to:

- raise attainment and improve behaviour and attendance in partnership schools;
- ensure personalisation of provision for children and young people, e.g. flexible 14–19 provision, alternative educational provision;
- deliver on the *Every Child Matters* outcomes in all partnership schools and through childcare and extended services;
- support workforce reform through contributing to the continuing professional development of staff at all levels across schools, and disseminating good practice.

Membership of EIPs is flexible and wide-ranging and includes, in addition to schools and pupil referral units (PRUs), FE colleges, work-based training providers, early years settings, business partners and sports clubs. The schools that can benefit the most from participating in an EIP are those that serve a distinct area of deprivation, those that most need affordable childcare and those that are already engaging in community issues.

Existing models of partnership working such as Leading Edge Partnerships, Networked Learning Communities, Federations and Learning Partnerships can be streamlined and built upon by EIPs.

Checklist for developing an Education Improvement Partnership

- ❑ **Define the common collective purpose underpinning joint activities.**
- ❑ **Be clear about what exactly the EIP wants to achieve and what will be done better together.**
- ❑ **Promote inclusion and encourage every school in the partnership to participate.**
- ❑ **Build upon the best of any successful local existing partnerships.**
- ❑ **Identify early on the readiness and contributions each school could make to the EIP.**
- ❑ **Share the vision collectively to create real sense of ownership and belonging to the EIP.**
- ❑ **Build teams across the EIP schools that promote, support and champion the EIP initiative.**
- ❑ **Develop clear channels of communication across the EIP.**
- ❑ **Be open, honest and transparent with the other partner organisations.**
- ❑ **Value and recognise the contributions of all schools and services in the EIP, giving each equal worth.**

- ❑ **Demonstrate a commitment to success for all children and young people.**
- ❑ **Where functions are being delegated from the LA to the EIP have a joint agreement (a service level agreement).**
- ❑ **Indicate how any joint agreement fits into the LA Children's and Young People's Plan and with Children's Trust arrangements.**
- ❑ **Ensure mutual accountability exists among members of the EIP for shared functions and for outcomes delivered.**

Funding Education Improvement Partnerships

There are a number of funding sources available to EIPs, which rely on partnership schools pooling some of their funding. Examples of typical funding sources that could be utilised are specialist schools community funding, leading schools and training schools money, School Sports Partnership funding and the Primary Strategy Learning Networks funding.

A group of schools themselves who are in a federation or a collegiate may agree to commit a percentage of their budget to a dedicated EIP fund. There will also be delegated LA funding for those EIPs who have been commissioned to take on LA service delivery functions.

Childcare, extended services and Education Improvement Partnerships

Education Improvement Partnerships bring together local providers from the private, voluntary or community sector, as well as from public health and social care agencies, to develop and build on services and activities.

Examples of such activities include establishing one-stop multi-agency centres, or a teenage information advice centre, on school sites, or networking extended provision across partnership schools for out-of-school-hours clubs or activities related to music, sport or art. The extended services provided by one or two schools in an EIP can be shared across the other schools in the partnership, e.g. the childcare offer.

Representatives from EIPs can become members of the Children's Trust board, or be on any working group reporting to it. These representatives from EIPs can help to shape and inform the trust's planning and commissioning strategies. The LA may commission an EIP to resolve a local problem, in partnership with other services and organisations.

Further information about EIPs can be found at:
www.standards.dfes.gov.uk/sie/si/educationimprovementpartnerships

Double click on the EIP link on title page, and you will find a drop down menu with various aspects of EIPs such as practicalities, case studies and EIP conferences 2005 and 2006. The webpage address for these conferences is: www.standards.dfes.gov.uk/sie/si/eips/eip_conference06

There are additional delegate handouts from the 2006 EIP Conference, which provides a model EIP Service Level Agreement and a model EIP Memorandum of Understanding.

Children's trusts

Children's trusts are partnerships between different organisations that provide, commission and deliver better outcomes for children and young people. Local authorities lead children's trusts strategically, with the Director of Children's Services being accountable for the services provided by the trust.

The LA children's services department will facilitate, encourage and support schools in its area to contribute to, and benefit from children's trust activity. They will also ensure that schools' views are sought and fed back. Trusts, working together with local partners, including headteachers, assess local needs, agree priorities and commission local services to meet those priorities.

Children's trust arrangements have four essential components:

- professionals are enabled and encouraged to work together in more integrated frontline services, built around the needs of children and young people;
- common processes are designed to create and underpin joint working;
- a planning and commissioning framework which brings together agencies' planning, supported by pooled budgets and resources to ensure key priorities, is identified and addressed;
- strong inter-agency governance arrangements with shared ownership, clear accountability and clear terms of reference are in place.

Children's trusts help to facilitate networking with other organisations by bringing together all services for children and young people in an area. They are responsive to local circumstances and need by brokering and commissioning multi-agency partnerships to deliver better outcomes for children and young people.

Children's trusts can help to develop and establish new ways of working, across services and organisations. They support those who work every day with children and young people and their families, from the Children's Workforce, from voluntary and community sector organisations, including teachers in schools and early years practitioners in children's centres.

Children's trusts provide an excellent opportunity for extended schools to strengthen and widen their remit of the extended services they provide. The new school profile gives extended schools the opportunity to set out clearly for parents, external partners and agencies the full range of services they offer. Extended schools can be commissioned by children's trusts to deliver integrated children's services, co-located on the site of a school. Find out more about children's trusts at: www.everychildmatters.gov.uk/aims/childrenstrusts/faq

Youth matters and children's trusts

While parents are the strongest influence in young people's lives, integrated services also have a key role to play in providing opportunities, challenge and support to teenagers. Schools will have an important part to play in delivering the local offer, through extended services to young people, in responding to the *Youth Matters* strategy. The government's vision is to see services integrated around young people's needs helping all teenagers to achieve the five *Every Child Matters* outcomes.

When planning and developing extended school and children's centre extended services and wrap-around care for young people, you will need to consider:

- how to engage young people in a wide range of positive recreational, cultural, sporting and enriching activities, empowering them to shape the services they receive;
- how to encourage more young people to volunteer and become involved in their communities;
- how to provide better information, advice and guidance to young people to help them make informed choices and decisions about their lives, careers, education and health;
- how to provide better and more personalised tailored intensive support for young people who have serious problems or who engage in trouble.

This means that any extended school services and activities provided for young people must:

- be responsive to what young people and their parents/carers want;
- balance greater opportunities and support with promoting young people's responsibilities;
- make young people's services more integrated, efficient and effective;
- improve outcomes for all young people, narrowing the gap between those who do well and those who don't;
- involve a wide range of organisations from the voluntary, community and private sectors to increase choice and secure the best outcomes;
- build on the best quality and impact of what is currently provided.

Local authorities, working through children's trusts, will be responsible for commissioning and producing activities and facilities for young people. The children's trust will:

- assess the needs of local young people;
- map existing services from the voluntary, private and public sectors against the needs of young people, to gap fill and avoid overlap;
- plan, through the Children and Young People's Plan, an integrated, responsive, accessible and effective range of services and provision;
- redesign services, informed by evidence, and commission provision to meet young people's needs, from a range of providers.

In addition, the children's trust will develop strong links with the Youth Offending Teams, local Learning and Skills Councils, the Russell Commission Implementation Body – a national framework for youth action and engagement from www.russellcommission.org and the Big Lottery Fund.

Further information about the government's strategy *Youth Matters*, and the role of children's trusts is to be found at: www.everychildmatters.gov.uk *Youth Work and Extended Services in Schools*, and YSQM Quality Mark for Services for Young People from the National Youth Agency website: www.nya.org.uk

Commissioning services

Commissioning refers to the process of assessing needs, allocating resources, defining priorities and choices and determining how they are best delivered.

Nine steps to joint planning and commissioning

- **Look at outcomes for children and young people in the local area to identify trends.**
- **Look at particular groups of children and young people.**
- **Develop an overall integrated needs assessment from users and staff views, as well as from data analysis.**
- **Identify available resources and set priorities for action, having agreed on the nature and scale of the local challenge.**
- **Plan a pattern of services most likely to secure priority outcomes.**
- **Decide how to commission (purchase or provide) services efficiently.**
- **Commission – including use of pooled resources and pooled budgets.**
- **Plan for workforce development and other changes in local processes and ways of working necessary to support service delivery.**
- **Monitor and review services and process.**

Joint commissioning involves partner agencies addressing issues together to decide:

- how best to meet identified needs, tested and led by the participation of children and young people, including how services can be designed to be outcome focused;

- how best to allocate and use collective resources of all kinds to secure those services from both statutory and non-statutory sources, against outcome-based targets;
- what agreements, contracts and monitoring arrangements need to be put in place to ensure effective delivery, and to influence future planning activity. Further information on commissioning is available at: www.everychildmatters.gov.uk/resources-and-practice/search/EP00025 and *Planning the commissioning of services* from ContinYou toolkit, email: info.coventry@continyou.org.uk

Productive partnerships

Partnerships entail a group of people joining together, sharing a common problem or issue and collectively taking responsibility for resolving it. *Every Child Matters* should be reflected in all partnership activity.

Partnership working involves:

- **co-operation** – partners sharing information and recognising the value of partnership working, i.e. pooling the collective knowledge, skills and achievements available;
- **co-ordination** – partners plan together to focus on a specific project, share some roles and responsibilities, resources and risk taking;
- **collaboration** – longer-term commitment between partners, with organisational changes that bring shared leadership, control, resources and risk taking.

You may engage internal partners, i.e. those who work in school, with families or in the community, or external partners, i.e. the LA, the voluntary service council, other schools or organisations.

Checklist for planning and developing partnership working

- **The aims, goals and key purpose of the partnership are clear.**
- **It is clear what all partners bring to the activity, project or service.**
- **Realistic expectations exist as to what the partnership can hope to achieve.**
- **Careful consideration has been given to partners' diversity, culture, sensitivities.**
- **Realistic targets, objectives and milestones have been set.**
- **Respective responsibilities of members of the partnership are clear.**
- **Outcomes from partnership working are monitored and evaluated and will bring the desired outcomes and results.**

Further information is available from the ContinYou toolkit entitled *Working in Partnership to Support Families*, and can be downloaded from: www.continyou.org.uk/content.php?CategoryID=579

Involving people from the local community in extended service provision

Children and young people are more likely to respect and appreciate their community the more they learn about it and interact with it and its members. For example, children from the School Council attending meetings of the local Neighbourhood Action Group can contribute to policy making to achieve better outcomes and facilities in the community.

Involving members of the community in out-of-school-hours learning activities, either as providers or participants, enables them to develop a better understanding of what the school and children's centre represents in the local area.

Appointing a 'Children's Champion' who lives in the local area, and who is not a member of the school staff, helps to break down access and participation barriers for those parents and families who may be unsure about joining in activities at the school or children's centre. Developing this type of community distributed leadership is just as important as developing similar leadership among the school and centre staff.

Similarly, developing a Parent Council or Parent Action Group to work closely with the School Council helps to strengthen and promote community spirit, and raise aspirations. Training to support the Community Champion and the Parent Council is important in order to ensure they obtain a clear understanding about the concept of the community and community values; they know what it means to be a community group or a community champion; they understand what an extended school/children's centre is, as well as their purpose within the community.

Whatever activities and services are offered as part of the extended service programme, the impact on the community for the benefit of the children and families must be evident. Thinking about what happens in the school and the community beyond 9.00a.m. to 4.00p.m. is important for raising expectations and broadening children and young people's horizons.

Holding regular community meetings which are chaired by the Extended School Manager or Head of the Children's Centre helps to give an update on activities and services offered, as well as providing a forum for parents and other members of the community to identify services they would like in the future.

In order to ensure parents engage in out-of-school-hours learning and other activities, it is important that they are clear about the purpose and objectives of family learning; that they know what the time limit is for any activities, e.g. a three-week or eight-week course requiring one hour attendance per week; and that childcare provision is made available during family learning time.

When engaging parents in out-of-school-hours learning activities it is useful to give them good reasons for participating at a time convenient to them. Providing feedback to parents on their achievements to show them they really make a difference to supporting their child's learning and well-being, as well as to improving their own life chances, is equally important. Developing transfer and transition activities as part of out-of-school-hours learning is also crucial, whereby older students from the local secondary school work with younger children from the children's centre and/or feeder primary school, and special school.

When seeking any volunteers to deliver extended service provision it is important to make them aware of the facilities, support and training you can offer them, in addition to clarifying what your expectations are from them. In order to build up a good rapport with partner providers, it is good practice to meet with them regularly as a group in order that any potential problems or issues can be overcome early.

Ensuring children and young people participating in out-of-school-hours clubs and activities appreciate the achievement of other children and adults joining them from other local schools or clubs is also important.

Thanking extended school/children's centre service providers including any volunteers and sponsors is vital. Holding an annual thank you party, and sending them letters of personal appreciation from the children and young people they worked with, ensures that they feel appreciated and valued.

Checklist for working with voluntary and community sector organisations

- ❑ There is a clear policy on the use of school/children's centre premises by voluntary groups and other organisations, which makes explicit principles, hire arrangements and procedures.
- ❑ The voluntary groups and organisations have signed a user agreement accepting the policy.
- ❑ There is an ethos policy in existence, which makes clear to all those voluntary community sector (VCS) organisations using the premises, the need for mutual respect, tolerance and understanding between the different organisations.
- ❑ There is a brochure available explaining booking procedures, hiring charges and the facilities available for VCS organisations.
- ❑ There is a known clear scale of charges published for the hire of the premises and resources.
- ❑ VCS organisations and groups have undertaken the appropriate CRB criminal records check on their staff, providing services and activities.
- ❑ VCS organisations are fully aware of the child protection and health and safety procedures when working in the organisation.
- ❑ There has been a careful check undertaken as to which organisations and groups are not able to use the premises because they contravene the local authority guidance and the aims of the school/centre.

(Adapted from ContinYou/DfES 2005c: 7–8)

Voluntary and community organisations benefit from the opportunity to:

- engage in the development and delivery of services for children, young people, families and communities;
- raise awareness about their services and activities;
- access school/children's centre facilities at a fair and reasonable cost.

Welcoming the whole community: customer care

Welcoming the whole community to the organisation is a core element of an inclusive ethos. The welcoming school/children's centre is evident by the respectful, courteous and helpful attitudes and behaviour of staff, children and young people towards visitors. The quality of the organisation's environment, the efficiency of administrative procedures and the clarity of communications are further evidence of a welcoming school or centre. A commitment to customer care supports continual improvement and self-evaluation.

Checklist for developing and implementing a customer care approach

- ❑ There are clear signs inside and outside the building to help visitors locate various areas in the school/centre.
- ❑ The reception area is welcoming, bright, cheerful and friendly.
- ❑ Reception staff and site management staff receive ongoing training in customer care, diversity and basic skills awareness.
- ❑ All staff are customer focused and responsive to customer needs, which helps to put visitors at their ease.
- ❑ There is an appropriate balance between security and customer care.
- ❑ Footpaths, entrances and car parks are well illuminated by external lighting, when it is dark.
- ❑ The premises are kept clean, free from litter and provide a pleasant healthy environment.
- ❑ There are well-maintained toilet facilities which visitors can access.
- ❑ There is childcare provision on site or nearby, where visitors can safely leave young children.
- ❑ There is adequate parking with reserved space for disabled visitors.
- ❑ The organisation and its facilities are accessible to the disabled.
- ❑ The school/centre is inclusive and welcoming to everyone.
- ❑ There are quality standards in place for responding to customer enquiries.

- ❑ **Complaints procedures are transparent and effective.**
- ❑ **Publicity and information materials are well produced, up-to-date and readily available in a range of formats and languages.**
- ❑ **There are clear procedures in place to deal with any customer/visitors who may become distressed, abusive or threatening.**
- ❑ **Regular site meetings are held to review and further develop community use, and discuss issues relating to welcoming visitors.**
- ❑ **There is an identified lead person on the staff with responsibility for implementing and reviewing the customer care policy.**

(ContinYou/DfES 2005d: 3–6)

The Charter Mark

The Charter Mark (a registered certification mark) is a national standard awarded to organisations and services who have achieved recognition for their excellence in customer service. A charge is made for gaining the Charter Mark.

This mark acts as a lever for change and improvement in service delivery, set against six key criteria. The Charter Mark, through a process of self-assessment, enables the extended school or children's centre to explore the answer to the fundamental question: 'What does the customer expect or hope for from the service(s) on offer?' There is an online self-assessment toolkit for school leaders and heads of children's centres to use to gain an initial overview of how the organisation is performing in relation to customer service, which also helps to identify any areas requiring further improvement. The most effective way to manage this self-assessment process in working towards achieving the Charter Mark is to adopt a team approach, whereby six individual staff each take responsibility for gathering evidence and reviewing progress towards meeting one of the six criteria. This information can then be brought together to begin a final assessment.

The six criteria against which customer service is assessed are:

1 set standards and perform well;
2 actively engage with your customers, partners and staff;
3 be fair and accessible to everyone and promote choice;
4 continuously develop and improve;
5 use your resources effectively and imaginatively;
6 contribute to improving opportunities and quality of life in the communities you serve.

Each of the six criteria have a set of sub-criteria, with suggested sources of evidence to meet each one. Criteria 6 enables the organisation in relation to community renewal and regeneration to be aware of the impact and potential usefulness of the service provision to the local community, particularly in enriching the social and/or economic life of the community.

The benefit of undertaking the initial online self-assessment is that it enables the school leader or head of children's centre to decide if they have sufficient evidence and are ready to formally apply for the Charter Mark. The value of achieving the Charter Mark is that it enables the local community to recognise that the organisation has earned a good reputation for the quality and excellence of the services and wrap-around care it provides on site.

The website to access the self-assessment toolkit is: www.chartermark.gov.uk
Successful extended schools and children's centres should:

- ❑ set clear service and performance standards by consulting customers, regularly reviewing progress towards meeting the standards

- ❑ actively engage and work with customers, partners and staff to ensure high-quality services are delivered
- ❑ consult with and involve present and potential customers, partners and staff
- ❑ communicate clearly with customers, using plain jargon-free language and a range of formats suited to customers' needs
- ❑ provide full information about services, their cost and how well they perform
- ❑ make services available to everyone who needs them, offering choice whenever possible
- ❑ treat everyone fairly in access to services and service delivery, particularly those who may have a disability or SEN
- ❑ learn from, and improve services, as a result of compliments, complaints and suggestions from customers
- ❑ have a clear, well-publicised and easy to use complaints procedure, with the opportunity for independent review wherever possible
- ❑ use resources effectively and imaginatively to provide best value.

(ContinYou/DfES 2005d: 6)

Further activities for school leaders and heads of children's centres

The following questions, based on aspects covered in this chapter, related to implementing and operating wrap-around care and extended services, will enable you to discuss and identify positive ways forward in meeting the government's Change for Children Programme.

- Which factors are important in promoting the take-up of services by members of the community?
- What key strategies will be utilised to protect the longer-term sustainability of services and extended activities?
- What opportunities exist for individuals within and outside the organisation to act as advocates in the local community, promoting services?
- What key new relationships need to be built?
- How will internal relationships within the organisation need to change in order to develop joined-up collaborative productive partnerships with external providers?
- What local plans and strategies can be used to develop shared partnerships to support longer-term extended school/children's centre initiatives?
- What strategies will be adopted to prevent a community dependency culture occurring in relation to service provision?
- Which services and activities does the organisation want to undertake in the short term, and why?
- How will you involve those from outside the school or children's centre in the planning and development process?
- What structures and additional capacity will be required to ensure that any longer-term services and extended activities are effective and have a positive impact on users?
- What are the key factors that help us work effectively with partners and providers of services?
- What are the main barriers faced in partnership working and how can these be removed and minimised?

5

Implementing *Every Child Matters* in Extended Schools and Children's Centres

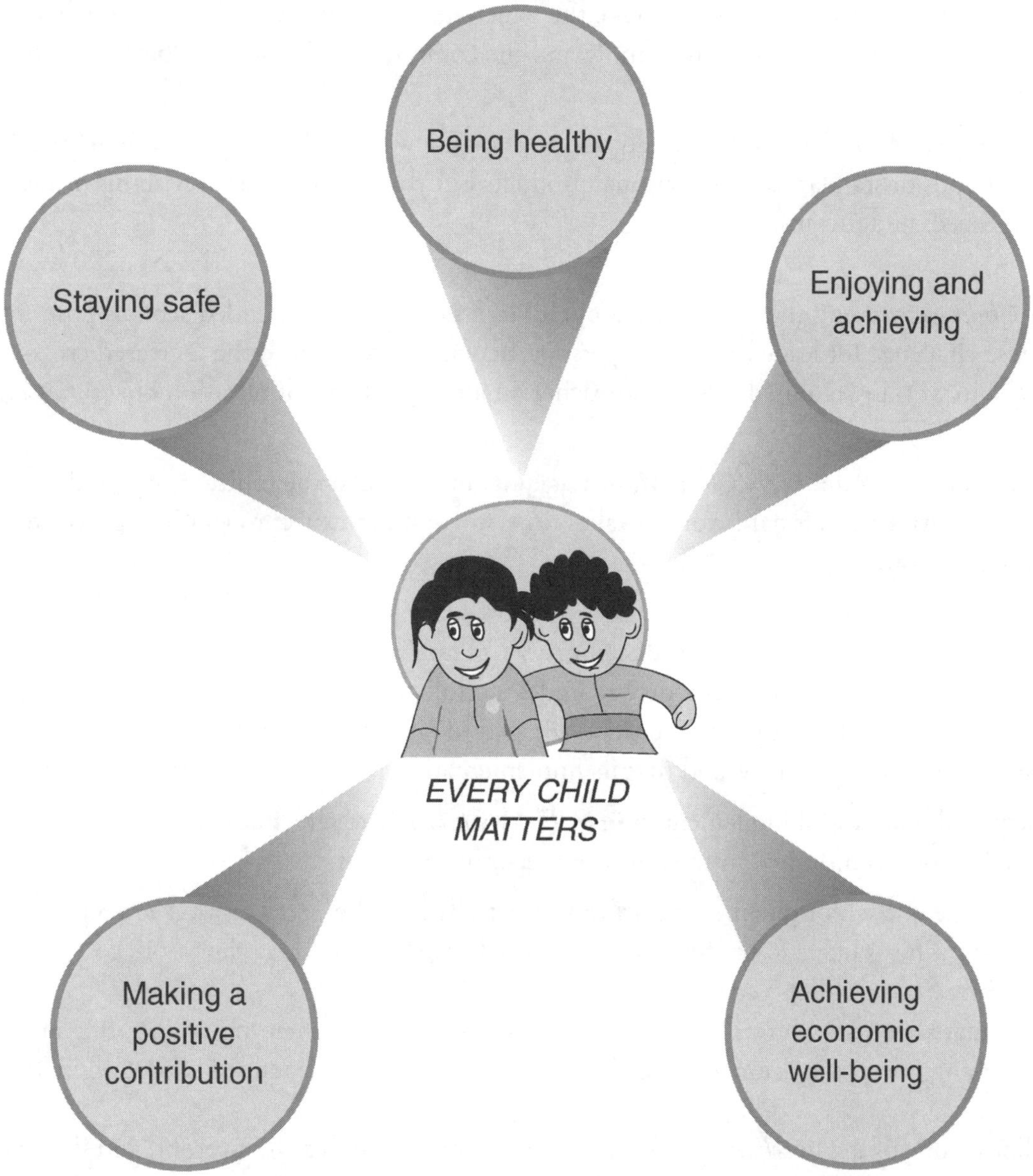

How to implement *Every Child Matters*

The government's ambitions set out in *Every Child Matters* are aimed at improving the outcomes for all children and young people, including the most disadvantaged, and those with additional needs, by intervening early to prevent things from going wrong in the first place. The philosophy behind the government's *Every Child Matters* change for children programme is to protect, nurture and improve the life chances of children and young people, in particular those of vulnerable children.

Central to the success of the *Every Child Matters* policy are children's centres and extended schools, acting as 'hubs' in the local community, offering differentiated personalised services for children and their families. Dame Pat Collarbone, Director of the National Remodelling Team, in her Speech at the Target 2010 Conference in November 2005, remarked:

> Within the framework of the *Every Child Matters* agenda, it is extended schools and children's centres which will have the biggest impact on the lives of children
>
> (p. 1)

In order to better understand the child and young person within the school context, extended schools and children's centres need to take the wider view, and give consideration to what life is like for their children outside, in the family and the community. Charles Leadbeater and Sarah Gillinson note:

> *Every Child Matters* is fundamentally about changing ways of thinking – children are not just pupils or standardised educational products but young people, each with his or her own needs and dreams.
>
> (NCSL, 2005c: 15).

Every Child Matters and the development of children's centres and extended schools pose an immense challenge for leaders and managers, particularly in relation to the increased cross-agency partnership working required. One headteacher, in a recent NCSL publication on *Every Child Matters* considered

> [i]mplementing the *Every Child Matters* agenda, in particular the multi-agency and community aspects is hard work, it takes time and you can expect to run into problems along the way.
>
> (NCSL 2006a: 13)

Unfortunately, the government introduced *Every Child Matters* without putting the necessary infrastructure of training and workforce remodelling fully in place first, in order to support capacity building. School leaders, in particular, need to take into account the fact that *Every Child Matters* is a long-term strategy, and that its implementation is an ongoing long-term process.

The key to the successful implementation of *Every Child Matters* in children's centres and extended schools is indicated in the following recommendations.

- Designate one senior member of staff to strategically lead the *Every Child Matters* policy and practice. This is likely to be the deputy headteacher in an extended school, or the head/deputy in a Sure Start children's centre.
- Nominate five staff who will each take responsibility for implementing, monitoring and evaluating one of the five *Every Child Matters* outcomes in the extended school or children's centre.
- Allocate one of the five *Every Child Matters* outcomes to a different governor, and link them to the nominated staff member to share the responsibility for monitoring and evaluating that particular outcome.

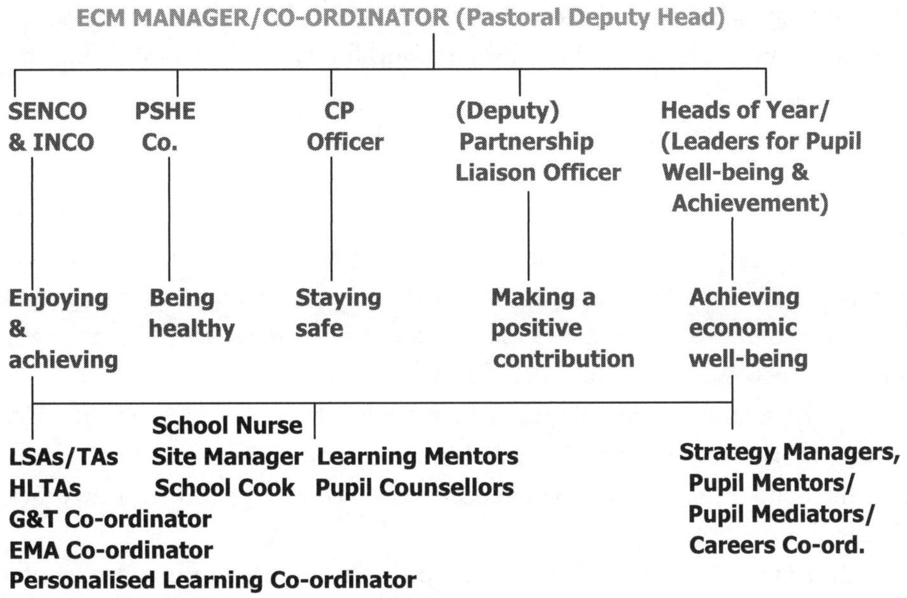

Figure 5.1 *Every Child Matters* Inclusion Team

- Form an *Every Child Matters* Focus Group whose membership should include: the headteacher or head of centre, deputy head and the five staff with an ECM outcome responsibility, representation from the governing body, representatives from children, pupils, as well as representation from non-teaching staff, i.e. teaching assistants, nursery nurses, learning mentor, parental representation. In addition include a representative from health and social care who work with the setting or school, and an external critical friend, who could be from another local school/children's centre, or a representative from the local authority. The group should meet formally at least once a term, with a specific focus. The outcomes and actions arising from these meetings should be fed back to the relevant stakeholders, and, in particular, connect with the multi-agency partners' meetings as well as to the extended school or children's centre service team meetings.
- In extended schools, nominate a pupil from every class in the school as an *Every Child Matters* representative, who takes responsibility for gathering the views of the class on aspects of the five *Every Child Matters* outcomes and how the school provision to meet these could be improved for pupils. This class representative will be responsible for feeding these views back to the School Council.
- Inform parents about the five *Every Child Matters* outcomes and their link to whole school/ centre policy and practice, including extended services. Survey their views annually on both these aspects.
- Display the *Every Child Matters* outcomes around the school/centre in communal areas, including teaching areas. Produce these outcomes in child-friendly language for younger children.
- Ensure both teaching and non-teaching staff refer to these outcomes when monitoring and evaluating the impact of any additional provision and services on children's learning and well-being outcomes.
- Review the school's/centre's mission statement to ensure that this reflects and makes reference to *Every Child Matters.*
- Ensure that the school/centre development plan features a priority(s) related to *Every Child Matters,* and that all subject and aspect development plans reflect this.
- Involve children in reviewing their own progress towards achieving the *Every Child Matters* outcomes by introducing a Children's ECM Profile/Log Book.

- Ensure that any staff training or information evenings for parents/carers include inputs from health and social care members of the children's workforce, who are supporting the school/ centre, to clarify their role.
- Seek opportunities as part of the workforce remodelling staffing restructuring to maximise upon staff expertise in aspects of *Every Child Matters* outcomes, e.g. Leading Learning Mentor for pupil well-being; Leading Teacher for pupil achievement and well-being; explore the advanced skills teacher (AST)/excellent Teacher route; Leading Early Years Practitioner.
- Look for opportunities to work in partnership with other neighbouring schools/centres to undertake joint activities and initiatives focused on improving an aspect of an *Every Child Matters* outcome, across a cluster or federation of schools.
- Ensure that all the school/centre policies make reference to the five *Every Child Matters* outcomes, as well as to any relevant extended activities and services provided.
- Ensure that the School Profile makes reference to the *Every Child Matters* outcomes and extended school provision.
- Ensure that the school's/centre's self evaluation provides evidence of the impact of additional provision and extended services on the outcomes for children and the community.
- Refer to the revised national standards for classroom teachers and review teachers' job descriptions to align them with and reflect the skills and knowledge of the Children's Workforce, as well as *Every Child Matters* outcomes and extended school/children's centre activities.
- Provide an *Every Child Matters* link on the school/centre website so as to provide information and updates on developments and progress.
- Hold showcase events for parents/carers, members of the community and other external multi-agency and local authority professionals, which celebrate the school's/centre's achievements in activities related to the *Every Child Matters* outcomes.
- Promote and publicise the school's/centre's best practice in *Every Child Matters* outcomes and activities in the community via the media, through local partnership and virtual networks.

Although *Every Child Matters* provides a coherent framework to enable schools to link achievement and well-being, there is some confusion as to whether it is intended for every child, or only those with additional needs. In addition, it has a tendency to operate on a deficit model.

Every Child Matters mission statement

In view of the government's change for children programme, it is timely for schools' and children's centres to review their mission statements in order to ensure they embrace *Every Child Matters* and extended service provision. Mission relates to the fundamental purpose for the existence of the organisation and its related services.

Any mission statement should express a view (vision), for the future, i.e. the long-term goal you are working towards, as well as the values and beliefs that govern how your organisation/service operates.

The mission statement for a children's centre or an extended school should be a simple, jargon-free memorable paragraph, which answers three key questions:

- the purpose of the organisation – what are the needs to be addressed?
- the business of the organisation – what are we doing to address those needs?
- the values of the organisation – what principles and beliefs guide our work?

A range of stakeholders need to contribute to the formulation of the mission statement by listing any relevant words, phrases or ideas under each of the three key questions. An effective mission statement motivates, inspires and supports ongoing commitment. The following two examples provide a model, which can be adapted and customised to suit the context of a children's centre or an extended school.

Extended school *Every Child Matters* mission statement

Step-by-step example:

The purpose: *every child matters* and everyone feels valued as a member of an inclusive, culturally diverse and enriching learning community
The business: offer accessible, good-quality extended school provision
The values: promote a sense of belonging, achievement and well-being for all

Model extended school mission statement

Maple School ensures that through its accessible good-quality extended school provision, planned in partnership with the community, *every child matters* and everyone feels valued as a member of an inclusive, culturally diverse and enriching learning community.

We believe the leisure activities, lifelong learning opportunities and the personalised services on offer to pupils, their families and the community promote a real sense of belonging, achievement and well-being for all.

Model children's centre mission statement

At Leafy Lane Children's Centre we are committed to providing accessible, fully inclusive, quality early education and childcare, family support, health services, employment advice and specialist support that meets the needs of children and families in the local community, and which fulfil the five *Every Child Matters* outcomes of: being healthy, staying safe, enjoying and achieving, making a positive contribution and achieving economic well-being.

Every Child Matters model policy

Statement of principle

Maple School ensures that through its accessible, good-quality extended services and activities *every child matters* and everyone feels valued as a member of a culturally diverse, enriching and inclusive learning community.

We believe the leisure activities, lifelong learning opportunities and the wrap-around care and personalised services on offer to pupils, families and the community promote a real sense of belonging and achievement, in fulfilling the *Every Child Matters* five outcomes for children of: being healthy, staying safe, enjoying and achieving, making a positive contribution, and achieving economic well-being.

This policy was developed in consultation and agreed with staff, governors, pupils, parents/carers and partners from multi-agency services, voluntary and community-sector organisations.

Aims

The extended school aims to:

- promote an ethos of belonging to the school and the wider local community;
- develop a sense of respect and responsibility among children, young people and adults within the school;

- enable all pupils to reach their optimum potential through the delivery of barrier-free personalised learning and personalised services which meet a diversity of needs;
- provide well-co-ordinated wrap-around care and extended services to support pupils and families in the community;
- provide an appropriate range of enriching, interesting and relevant out-of-school-hours learning activities that respond to identified needs;
- develop collaborative and productive partnerships with other schools, public and private service providers that meet the *Every Child Matters* outcomes
- promote the achievement and well-being of pupils, families and the community accessing the extended services;
- work in partnership with parents/carers to enable them to support the learning and well-being of their child;
- demonstrate value added progress on the five *Every Child Matters* outcomes through the use of appropriate assessment such as the Personal and Social Development Scale, the Emotional and Behavioural Development Scale, and the Personal, Social, Health Education and Citizenship assessment criteria;
- challenge discrimination and celebrate diversity.

Objectives

Being healthy

Ensure pupils:

- engage with the Healthy Schools Programme to benefit from a healthy lifestyle;
- participate in PE and other forms of sport and exercise;
- eat and drink healthily within school;
- benefit from on-site health and social care services to support their emotional, mental and physical well-being.

Staying safe

Ensure pupils are:

- safe, free from bullying, harassment and discrimination;
- provided with a safe environment in which to develop, learn, play and socialise with others.

Enjoying and achieving

Ensure pupils:

- experience good-quality, fully inclusive teaching and learning;
- actively participate in enjoyable, relevant, interesting learning and recreational activities within and beyond the school day;
- regularly attend and enjoy school;
- review their own progress and any additional provision, which includes tailored teaching, catch-up or extension activities;
- are well supported during periods of transition and transfer between and within schools.

Making a positive contribution

Ensure pupils:

- engage in decision making, good behaviour, develop positive relationships, self-confidence and can manage change;

- have the opportunity to take responsibility in school, e.g. peer mentor, study buddy, peer mediator, prefect, form representative on School Council
- have a say in how the extended school and its related services operate
- have the opportunity to participate in activities within the local community and between other schools
- are well supported in developing socially and emotionally.

Achieving economic well-being

Ensure pupils:

- have the opportunity to participate in 'Young Enterprise' activities;
- acquire key skills in relation to communication, team work, co-operative learning, financial awareness, problem solving and work-related learning.

Concept of Every Child Matters

Every Child Matters, the government's change for children programme, identifies that pupil performance and well-being go hand in hand. Children and young people cannot learn effectively if they do not feel safe or if health problems create barriers to learning.

Every Child Matters protects, nurtures and improves the life chances of children and young people, particularly of those who are vulnerable or at risk of underachieving.

The five outcomes of *Every Child Matters*: (being healthy, staying safe, enjoying and achieving, making a positive contribution, and achieving economic well-being) are central to ensuring that effective joined-up children's services from education, health and social care are provided on or near the site of the school.

The extended school ensures that the *Every Child Matters* outcomes for children are met as part of the Children Act 2004.

Relationship with other policies

Extended school policy
Inclusion policy
Equal opportunities policy
Admissions policy
Safeguarding/child protection policy
SEN policy and school accessibility plan
Behaviour policy
Health and safety policy
Personal, social, health education and Citizenship policies
Personalised learning policy

Co-ordination

The headteacher has responsibility for ensuring that the *Every Child Matters* policy is fully implemented.

The deputy headteacher, responsible for pupil achievement and well-being, has overall responsibility for co-ordinating, monitoring and evaluating the effectiveness of the *Every Child Matters* policy and provision throughout the school. They oversee the five key staff designated with responsibility for leading the implementation, monitoring and review of one of the allocated five *Every Child Matters* outcomes, whole school. The deputy headteacher reports on the progress made towards meeting the five *Every Child Matters* outcomes for children and young people and the related priorities on the school development plan to the governing body. All teaching and non-teaching staff, including practitioners from multi-agency services, working with pupils within the school are responsible for ensuring children and young people achieve positive outcomes in relation to learning and well-being.

Implementation

- Specific attention will be paid to identifying and meeting the needs of pupils who are achieving poorly on the *Every Child Matters* outcomes;
- Staff will be sensitive to the needs of the whole child, and to relevant community issues;
- The school will promote pupil well-being within the school and in the wider local community;
- Pupils will be encouraged to share their worries and fears in an emotionally secure environment, with trusting adults;
- Information to parents/carers and the local community on *Every Child Matters* will be produced in a range of alternative formats and languages.

Monitoring and review

The *Every Child Matters* policy will be reviewed annually at the end of each academic year, to assess its effectiveness on pupils' well-being outcomes. Policy evaluation will focus on: establishing how far the aims and objectives of the policy have been met; how effectively resources have been allocated to meet the *Every Child Matters* outcomes; the progress pupils have made towards achieving the five *Every Child Matters* outcomes; as well as seeking the views of parents/carers, pupils, staff and other key stakeholders. In light of all this evidence, the policy will be revised accordingly.

Key dates

Ratification of the policy

Headteacher signature: ______________________________ Date: __________

Chair of Governors signature: __________________________ Date: __________

Policy implemented on: ____________________ Policy review date: ______________

Audit and review of *Every Child Matters*

School leaders and heads of centres will wish to confirm the current position within the organisation, in meeting the *Every Child Matters* outcomes, through a process of audit and self-review. Using the SWOT or solution-focused force field analysis is a good starting point for auditing *Every Child Matters* with the staff and governors.

The initial audit will help to identify the key priorities and actions to be included in the school or centre development plan. An example of a development plan, linking extended service provision to the *Every Child Matters* outcomes, is included in this section, for reference.

Two suggested review frameworks (Tables 5.2 and 5.3) and a model for reviewing *Every Child Matters* are provided (Figure 5.2), both of which help to formulate the development plan priorities, in addition to reviewing progress towards achieving the expected outcomes.

The review tools provided complement and support the OFSTED self-evaluation process. There are a number of other commercially produced self-evaluation frameworks which cover the *Every Child Matters* outcomes, for example, the Inclusion Quality Mark, Ensuring *Every Child Matters* Diagnostic and Planning Tool and the Cambridge Education Audit Tool. Seeking the views of service users (children and parents) is important in any review of *Every Child Matters* outcomes. A model pupil well-being log and a stakeholders survey are included at the end of this section. These can be customised and adapted to suit the context of the school or children's centre.

Table 5.1 SWOT analysis for *Every Child Matters*

SWOT ANALYSIS	
Every Child Matters aspect(s) to be addressed:	
STRENGTHS	**WEAKNESSES**
OPPORTUNITIES	**THREATS**

Table 5.2 Force Field Analysis framework for *Every Child Matters*

<table>
<tr><th colspan="2">FORCE FIELD ANALYSIS</th></tr>
<tr><td colspan="2">The change required for Every Child Matters:</td></tr>
<tr><th>FORCES SUPPORTING CHANGE</th><th>FORCES PREVENTING CHANGE</th></tr>
<tr><td></td><td></td></tr>
<tr><th colspan="2">STRATEGIES FOR SUSTAINABLE CHANGE IMPLEMENTATION OF EVERY CHILD MATTERS:</th></tr>
<tr><td colspan="2"></td></tr>
</table>

Table 5.3 *Every Child Matters* model review framework

	HEALTHY	SAFE	ENJOY & ACHIEVE	POSITIVE CONTRIBUTION	ECONOMIC WELL-BEING
Where are we now?					
Where do we want to go?					
How will we get there?					
What do we have to do?					

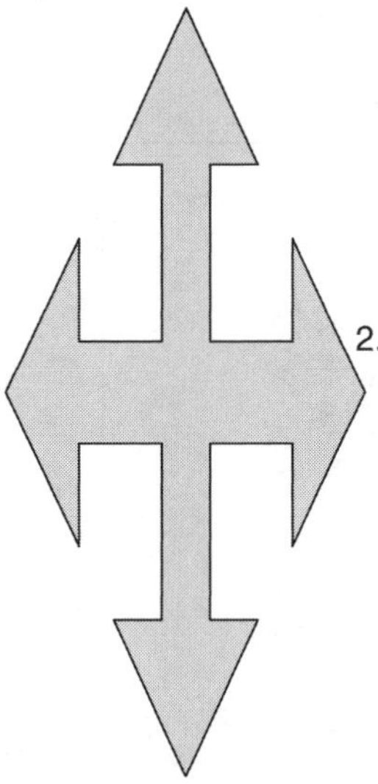
1. Current position on Every Child Matters
Where are we now?
What evidence do we have?
4. Evaluating progress
Outcomes achieved?
Impact of Every Child Matters?
What next?
2. Action planning
How to improve?
Action to take?
Action when, by whom?
Resources required
Expected outcomes
3. Acting on the plan
Are agreed actions happening?
How do we know?
Progress checks

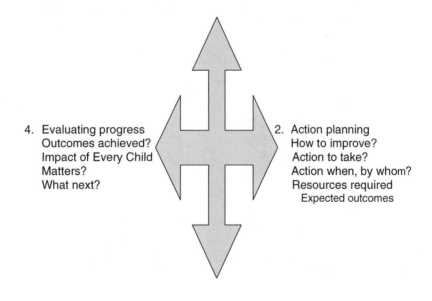

Figure 5.2 Model for reviewing *Every Child Matters* progress

Table 5.4 *Every Child Matters* and extended school development plan

Priority area	Activities	ECM outcomes	Lead person	Resources	Timescale	Outcomes/Impact
Childcare	(i) develop a breakfast club (ii) develop a charging policy for the club	Be healthy Enjoy and achieve	Lead teaching assistant	Fees Start up money from Standards Fund 2 parent volunteers	Planning June–July 07 Commences Sept. 07	Improved readiness for learning. Improved pupil punctuality and attendance at school.
Youth services	(i) provide summer holiday sports activities	Be healthy Enjoy and achieve Make a positive contribution	Community youth leader	Fees PESSCL funding Sponsorship from local football club 2 sports coaches	Planning June-July 07 Activities run from July to August 07 of the summer holidays	Reduced occurrence of anti-social teenage behaviour during school holidays in community. Increased pupil motivation and self-confidence.
Out-of-school hours learning	(i) develop and provide a multi-media club	Enjoy and achieve Make a positive contribution	Extended School co-ordinator	Standards Fund start-up money Fees Parent Volunteer from local TV company	Commissioning and planning – November–December 07 to commence January 08	Club oversubscribed. CD of school extended school activities produced.
Access to specialist services	(i) establish a pupil counselling service (ii) provide speech and language therapy	Be healthy Enjoy and achieve	Leader for pupil well-being to commission services	Health service funds School funding to buy in extra time from school nurse and CAMHS worker	Commissioning services in July 07 To start from September 07 academic year	Improved pupil mental health and well-being among critical groups. Improved pupil behaviour.
Support for parents	(i) provide family learning for fathers	Enjoy and achieve (supporting and promoting their child's learning & well-being)	Family support worker and the Family liaison co-ordinator	Funding for Family Learning from LSC	Activities to commence in April 07 (rolling programme of 6 weekly sessions)	Increased interest and participation by fathers in supporting their child's learning.
Community use	(i) develop a cyber café (ii) develop family first aid classes	Make a positive contribution Achieve economic well-being Stay safe	ICT technician from school School nurse	Fees Start-up sponsorship from local ICT company ICT technician time School Nurse time	Planning during May and June 07 Club commences in September 07 and will run for academic year	Oversubscribed. Enhanced community relationships with school. Some adults found work by using cyber café ICT.

Table 5.5 *Every Child Matters* Outcomes and Extended Services

Core offer aspect	Be healthy	Stay safe	Enjoy & achieve	Positive contribution	Economic well-being
Childcare					
Youth services					
Out-of-school-hours learning					
Access to specialist services					
Support for parents					
Community use					

List current extended school activities under each ECM outcome to provide an overview of coverage.

Table 5.6 *Every Child Matters* model pupil self-review well-being log

This well-being log belongs to: ______________________

Class/Form: ______________________

The five *Every Child Matters* well-being outcomes are:

Being healthy 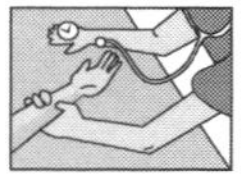

Staying safe 

Enjoy learning & achieving 

Positive contribution 

Achieving economic well-being 

Table 5.6 *(Continued)*

Being healthy 

Put a ✓ in the relevant box/boxes

How do you keep healthy in school?

exercise PE, sport ☐ eating & drinking healthy ☐ keeping hands clean ☐ manage own feelings ☐

What else do you need to do to stay healthy in school?

____

____

What do you do to have a healthy lifestyle outside school?

____

____

Who can help you to stay healthy?

(a) at school? ______________________________

(b) at home? ______________________________

What is your personal target for being healthy?

____

____

How will you achieve this target?

____

____

Staying safe 

Put a ✓ in the relevant box/boxes

How do you keep safe in school?

report bullying ☐ learn & play safely ☐ keep away from unsafe areas ☐ report any strangers to staff ☐

follow school fire drill ☐ look after the safety of others ☐

What else do you need to do to keep safe in school?

____

____

What do you do to keep safe outside school?

____

____

Who can help you stay even safer?

(a) at school? ______________________________

(b) at home? ______________________________

What is your personal target for staying safe?

____

____

How will you achieve this target? ______________________________

____

Table 5.6 *(Continued)*

Enjoying learning and achieving

Put a ✓ in the relevant box/boxes

How do you enjoy learning and achieving in school?

- learning in a group or pair ☐
- using favourite learning style ☐
- present work in other way to writing ☐
- value help of staff ☐
- enjoy going to school ☐
- like learning new things ☐
- behaving sensibly ☐
- attend school clubs ☐

What else do you need to do to enjoy learning and achieve in school?

______

What do you do to enjoy learning and to achieve outside school?

______

Who can help you to learn and achieve

(a) at school? ______

(b) at home? ______

What is your personal target for enjoying learning and achieving?

______

How will you achieve this target? ______

Making a positive contribution

Put a ✓ in the relevant box/boxes

How do you make a positive contribution in school?

- express views to School Council ☐
- helping others ☐
- partake in school events ☐
- school prefect ☐
- study buddy ☐
- sensible citizen ☐
- form/class representative ☐
- partake in after-school clubs ☐

What else do you need to do to make a positive contribution in school?

______

What do you do to make a positive contribution at home and/or in the local community?

______

Who can help you to make more of a positive contribution

(a) at school? ______

(b) at home/in the community? ______

What is your personal target for making a positive contribution?

______

How will you achieve this target?

______

Table 5.6 *(Continued)*

Achieving economic well-being 

Put a ✓ in the relevant box/boxes

How do you achieve economic well-being in school?

team working ☐ make sensible decisions ☐ look for new chances ☐ manage money ☐

use ICT ☐ idea about a career ☐ solve problems ☐

What else do you need to do to achieve economic well-being in school?

______

______

What do you do to achieve economic well-being outside school?

______

______

Who can help you to achieve economic well-being

(a) at school? ______

(b) at home? ______

What is your personal target for achieving economic well-being? ______

______

How will you achieve this target? ______

______

Self-review of the five well-being outcomes

Rate your overall progress in achieving the five well-being outcomes on a scale 1–3
(1 = a little progress; 2 = average progress; 3 = good progress)

Being healthy ☐ Making a positive contribution ☐

Staying safe ☐ Achieving economic well-being ☐

Enjoying learning and achieving ☐

Which well-being outcome do you need to improve in the most?

______

______

What will you need to do to enable you to achieve this well-being outcome?

______

______

Who can help you to achieve this well-being outcome

(a) at school? ______

(b) at home? ______

My overall main personal well-being target is:

______

______

Date of self-review ______

Signature ______

Seeking stakeholders' views on *Every Child Matters*

Stakeholders' survey on *Every Child Matters*

The government's five *Every Child Matters* outcomes for children and young people to be met by schools/children's centres are:

- Being healthy
- Staying safe
- Enjoying and achieving
- Making a positive contribution
- Achieving economic well-being

We value your views on the progress we are making towards meeting the five *Every Child Matters* outcomes.

Please answer the questions below and return this survey to the school or children's centre office.

QUESTIONS

1. Do you consider the school/centre makes the five *Every Child Matters* outcomes clear to children, staff, parents, governors, external agencies?
   YES ☐ NO ☐

   If no, what more could be done to improve this issue?

2. Do you consider you have the opportunity to express your views and opinions about how the school/centre intends to implement the *Every Child Matters* outcomes?
   YES ☐ NO ☐

   If no, please indicate how you would wish to have more of a say in this aspect?

3. Is there any particular *Every Child Matters* outcome that you would wish to see further developed or improved in the school/centre?
   YES ☐ NO ☐

   If yes, please indicate the *Every Child Matters* outcome:

   Suggest how this outcome could be best met within the school/centre.

4. The extended school activities and/or children's centre wrap-around services are designed to improve the *Every Child Matters* outcomes for children. Which other extended activities or wrap-around services would you wish to see put in place at the school or children's centre?

Thank you for taking the time to complete this survey.

Figure 5.3 Stakeholders' survey on *Every Child Matters*

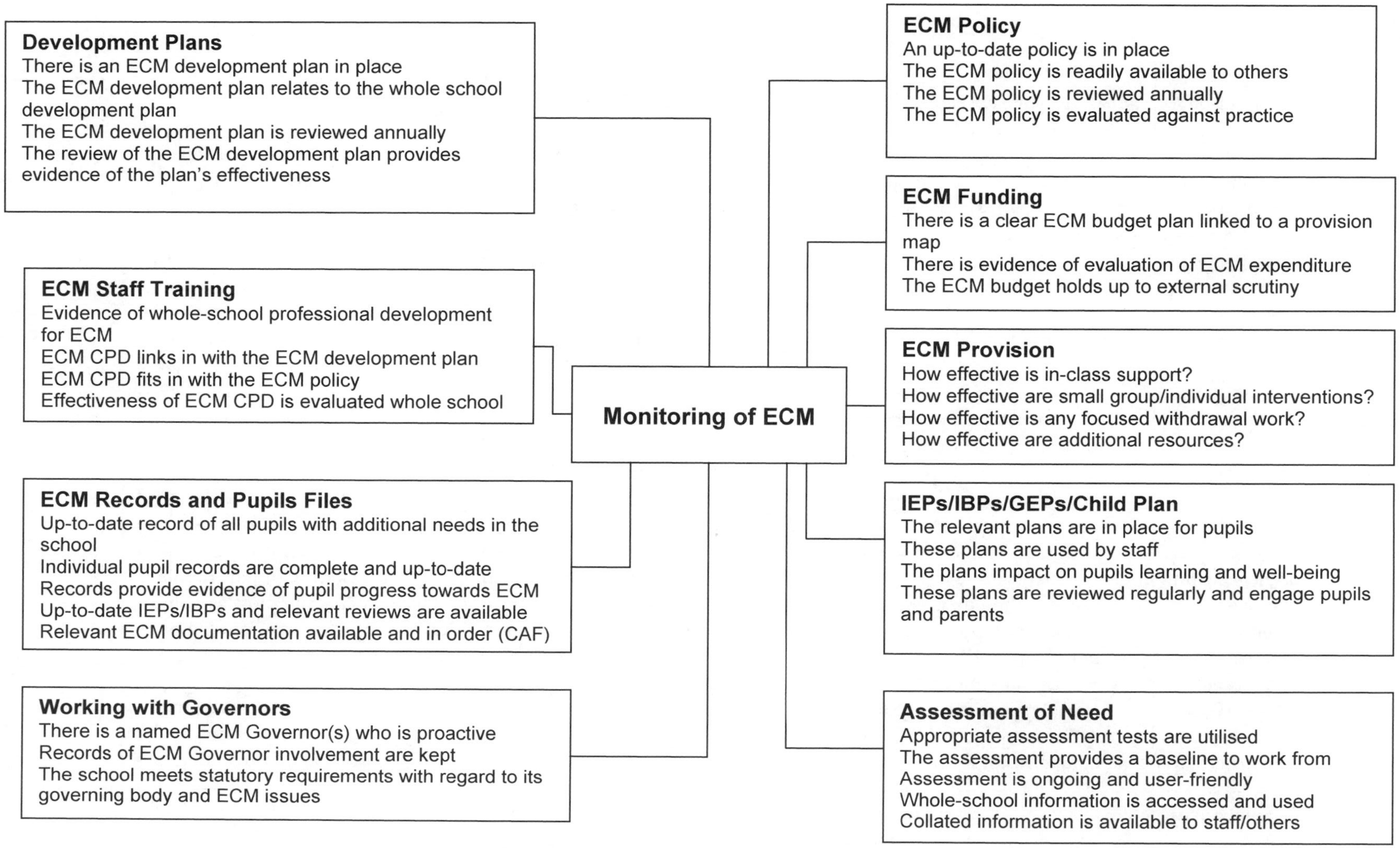

Development Plans
There is an ECM development plan in place
The ECM development plan relates to the whole school development plan
The ECM development plan is reviewed annually
The review of the ECM development plan provides evidence of the plan's effectiveness
ECM Staff Training
Evidence of whole-school professional development for ECM
ECM CPD links in with the ECM development plan
ECM CPD fits in with the ECM policy
Effectiveness of ECM CPD is evaluated whole school
ECM Records and Pupils Files
Up-to-date record of all pupils with additional needs in the school
Individual pupil records are complete and up-to-date
Records provide evidence of pupil progress towards ECM
Up-to-date IEPs/IBPs and relevant reviews are available
Relevant ECM documentation available and in order (CAF)
Working with Governors
There is a named ECM Governor(s) who is proactive
Records of ECM Governor involvement are kept
The school meets statutory requirements with regard to its governing body and ECM issues
Monitoring of ECM
ECM Policy
An up-to-date policy is in place
The ECM policy is readily available to others
The ECM policy is reviewed annually
The ECM policy is evaluated against practice
ECM Funding
There is a clear ECM budget plan linked to a provision map
There is evidence of evaluation of ECM expenditure
The ECM budget holds up to external scrutiny
ECM Provision
How effective is in-class support?
How effective are small group/individual interventions?
How effective is any focused withdrawal work?
How effective are additional resources?
IEPs/IBPs/GEPs/Child Plan
The relevant plans are in place for pupils
These plans are used by staff
The plans impact on pupils learning and well-being
These plans are reviewed regularly and engage pupils and parents
Assessment of Need
Appropriate assessment tests are utilised
The assessment provides a baseline to work from
Assessment is ongoing and user-friendly
Whole-school information is accessed and used
Collated information is available to staff/others

Figure 5.4 Monitoring *Every Child Matters* whole school. Adapted from D. Constable (2002) *Planning and Organising the SENCO Year.* London: David Fulton.

Table 5.7 Evaluating *Every Child Matters* five outcomes for children

ECM Outcomes	Outstanding 1	Good 2	Satisfactory 3	Inadequate 4
Be healthy	Developing healthy lifestyles is a high priority. Very good provision for and participation in physical activities. Health education valued and believed in by pupils. Very good opportunities exist for healthy eating and drinking. High levels of care alert staff to learners with problems and these are dealt with adeptly. Learners make very good progress in learning to recognise stress. School's support for learners in trouble is very good. Pupils' self-esteem is very good.	Majority of learners undertake 2 hours of organised PE, sport per week. School has well-organised and well-received health, drugs and sex education programmes. Good facilities exist on site for eating and drinking healthily. Lunches offer a balanced diet and vending machines contain healthy options. Staff are alert to the well-being of learners. Learners make good progress in recognising and dealing with stress and feel they can easily get support from staff when needed.	Great majority of learners undertake at least 2 hours of PE, sport per week. School has in place a satisfactory programme for health education, including drugs and sex education. Facilities exist for learners to eat and drink healthily on site. Learners are taught to recognise symptoms relating to a lack of mental well-being and have access to support when needed. Staff have adequate support to enable them to recognise health problems and refer them appropriately.	The curriculum and facilities do not adequately promote a healthy life style. Significant no. of learners don't have 2 hours of organised PE, sport per week. Health education provision, including that for drugs and sex, are deficient in range. Adequate facilities do not exist for learners to eat and drink healthily on site, or they are not encouraged sufficiently to do so. Distressed learners do not have their needs adequately supported. Pupils' self-esteem is very low.
Stay safe	Safety of learners is a very high priority. Risk assessments make learning activities safe. Learners feel very safe and know that they are very well supported when threatened by any form of intimidation. Pupils undertake all physical activities in a very orderly and sensible manner.	Good all-round approach to ensuring learners stay safe. Child protection procedures are clear and effective. Risk assessments are thorough and result in effective action. Learners feel safe. Pupils make good use of systems to report bullying, racism, harassment, and staff act decisively to protect them. Learners are taught to play sports safely.	Reasonable steps are taken to ensure safety of all learners. Child protection arrangements are in place. Staff undertake adequate risk assessments and act effectively upon them, making sure that dangerous materials and medicines are secure. Learners feel safe, and know and make use of reporting system for bullying. Pupils are taught to swim.	Provider does not take adequate steps to ensure that learners are safe. Learners don't feel safe. Lack of adequate child protection arrangements. Learners are exposed to unacceptable risks, resulting from inadequate risk assessment. Reporting systems for bullying are ineffective. Learners report they don't feel safe.

Table 5.7 *(Continued)*

ECM Outcomes	Outstanding 1	Good 2	Satisfactory 3	Inadequate 4
Enjoy and achieve	Standards are rising very fast or being maintained at very high levels. Virtually all learners make very good progress and enjoy learning very much. Personal development is very good, as shown in their high self-esteem, high aspirations and increasing independence. High-quality provision and teaching exist.	Standards are rising fast and compare well with similar schools. Learners make good progress and no significant groups lag behind. Pupils enjoy their education a great deal and have positive attitudes and good behaviour. Learners make good progress in their personal qualities. Provision and teaching are of good quality. Strengths and weaknesses are known and also what must be done to improve.	Standards are rising steadily and are broadly in line with those in similar schools. Most learners make at least satisfactory progress in the majority of subjects, courses and areas of learning. No group of learners underachieves significantly. Pupils generally enjoy their learning as shown by their satisfactory attitudes, behaviour and attendance. The personal development of most learners is satisfactory. The teaching, curriculum, recreational activities and monitoring of progress are satisfactory overall. Groups in difficulty are identified and there are adequate strategies to assist them.	Significant numbers of learners do not enjoy their education and or do not achieve adequately. The quality of provision or the effectiveness of management are inadequate to make the outcomes satisfactory. A significant number of pupils display disaffection. There are marked deficiencies in one or more aspects of learners' personal development. Provision and teaching are unsatisfactory. There is a lack of accurate self-evaluation and ineffective action arising from this.
Make a positive contribution to community	Learners make a very strong contribution to the community. Pupils are taught about their rights and encouraged and empowered to express their views very effectively. There is a self-disciplined community in which bullying and discrimination is very rare, and when it occurs is dealt with most effectively. Learners' views are central to the decisions made by the school. Learners have a very high level of involvement in community activities. Citizenship is a very strong part of the taught curriculum and in the life of the pupils.	Learners make a good contribution to the community. They have a clear understanding of their rights, a confidence to express their views and form constructive relationships with adults. Bullying and discrimination are rare and are dealt with effectively. Pupils' views are listened to and they are actively involved in activities that affect the community Citizenship is well embedded in the curriculum.	Learners have a satisfactory understanding of their rights and a reasonable understanding of how to bring about change. The incidence of bullying and discrimination is not high. Learners express their points of view, and several activities are initiated and managed by them. Adequate steps are taken to listen to the views of pupils, help them to form positive relationships with adults and take on responsibility. Clear policies exist to combat bullying and harassment, action is taken to reduce incidents of them and victims have good access to support.	Learners don't make an adequate contribution to their community and are not sufficiently encouraged to do so. Pupils have an inadequate understanding of their rights and participation in decisions that affect them. There is extensive bullying and discrimination. There is a low level of pupil involvement in communal activities. Significant shortfalls exist in the citizenship curriculum. There are inadequate mechanisms and action to deal with bullying and harassment.

Table 5.7 *(Continued)*

ECM Outcomes	Outstanding 1	Good 2	Satisfactory 3	Inadequate 4
Achieve economic well-being	High priority is given to developing the self-confidence skills of pupils. Challenging teaching styles and a wide range of engaging and demanding activities enable learners to make very good progress in their capacity to handle change and take initiative. Pupils make confident strides in their financial literacy. The area is most carefully monitored and imaginatively developed.	Learners make good progress in acquiring the skills and qualities that will enable them to do well at work. The teaching styles and available activities effectively promote enterprising qualities in learners. Financial literacy is a strong part of the curriculum and pupils progress well. The provision for this area of the curriculum is carefully monitored and continuously improved.	Learners acquire, as appropriate for their age, the skills and personal qualities that will enable them to succeed at work. A range of teaching styles and enrichment opportunities, satisfactorily promote these skills and qualities. Pupils make satisfactory progress in their financial literacy. The quality of work-related learning is reviewed accurately and adequate action is taken to remedy any weaknesses.	Learners don't make adequate progress in the skills and personal qualities that will enable them to succeed at work. There is slow progress made in acquiring work related skills. Teaching styles are overly didactic and don't enable pupils to develop their personal qualities and skills or their enterprise capability. Major gaps exist in KS4 provision.

Further activities for school leaders and heads of children's centres

The following questions based on aspects covered in this chapter related to implementing and embedding *Every Child Matters* will enable you to discuss and identify ways forward in meeting the government's change for children programme.

- What particular features of your school/centre currently make *Every Child Matters* outcomes a strength?
- What progress has already been made in beginning to address and respond to the five *Every Child Matters* outcomes strategically?
- What barriers exist in your school/centre that are inhibiting the full and successful implementation of *Every Child Matters*?
- What action needs to be taken to remove these barriers in order to make your school/centre even more *Every Child Matters* friendly?
- Who do you need to work with within the school/centre in order to implement and deliver the *Every Child Matters* outcomes successfully?
- Who else do you need to work with from outside the school/centre to help support you in implementing the *Every Child Matters* outcomes?
- How do you intend to monitor and evaluate the progress made in enabling children and young people to achieve the *Every Child Matters* outcomes?

6

Leadership and Management of Extended Schools and Children's Centres

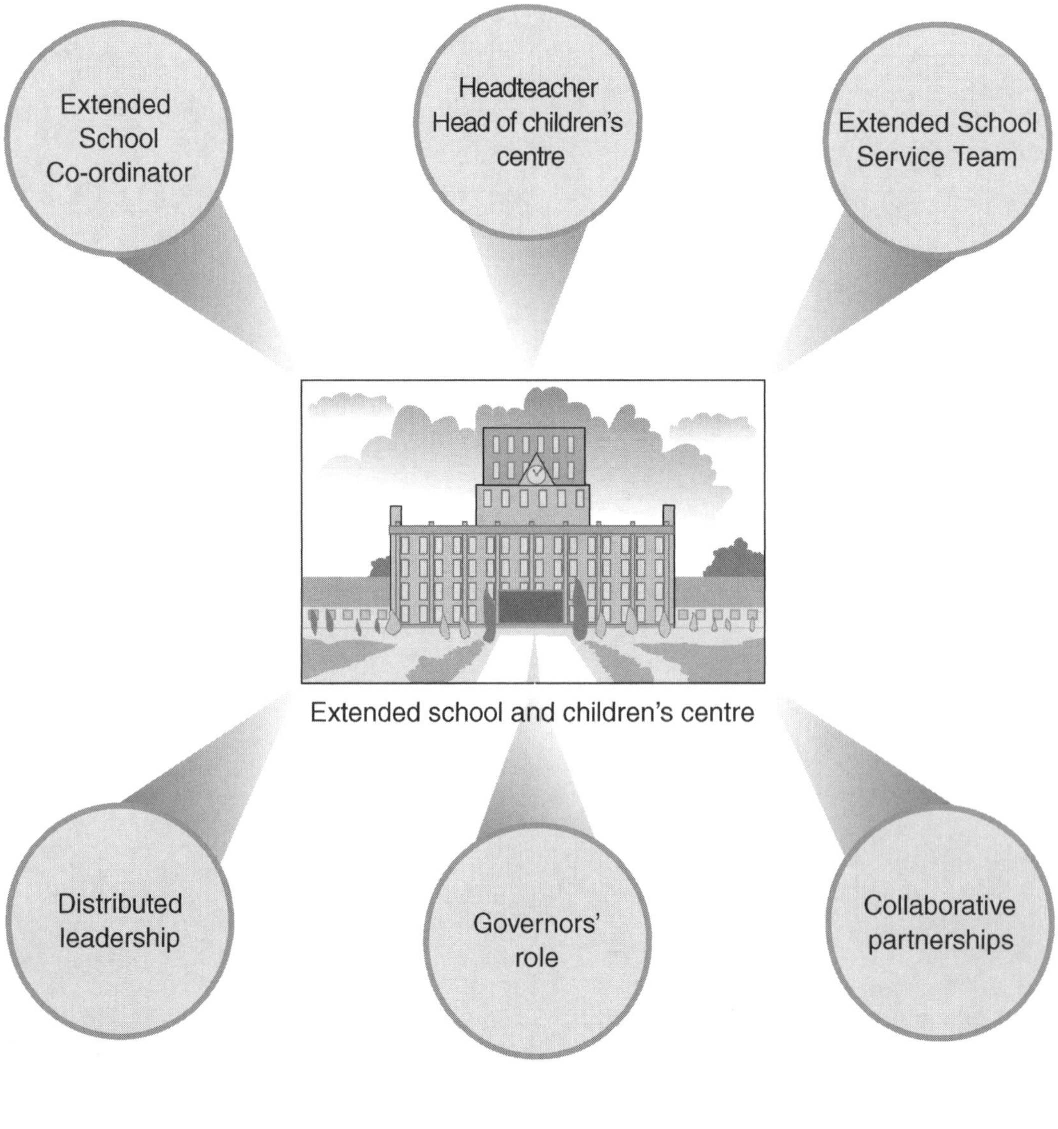

Leadership of extended school service provision

Under workforce remodelling and the National Agreement, there is no expectation that headteachers alone are to be responsible for managing extended services. Dedicated leadership and management structures for extended schools, which are not entirely reliant on the energies of the headteacher, are essential. The Office for Standards in Education (OFSTED), in their report on extended schools recommended that headteachers of newly designated extended schools:

> delegate more and do so earlier rather than later, to ensure that responsibilities are shared more equitably.
>
> (OFSTED 2005: 19)

In July 2006 OFSTED commented:

> Where co-ordinators for extended services were in place, headteachers reported no significant increase in their workload as a consequence of providing extended services.
>
> (OFSTED 2006c: 10)

The role of the extended school co-ordinator

The appointment of an extended school co-ordinator is essential for the successful development and delivery of extended services within a school. Usually, a deputy headteacher or the headteacher takes responsibility for line managing the extended school co-ordinator. They will also oversee his/her performance management and continuing professional development. The following job description and person specification provides a suggested model, which can be customised and adapted to suit the particular context of the school.

Job description

Post title: Extended School Co-ordinator
Hours: Full-time/Part-time
Responsible to: Deputy Headteacher (Pupil Services – achievement & well-being)
Purpose: To be responsible for the management and co-ordination of high-quality extended school services that meet the *Every Child Matters* outcomes for children.

Main duties and responsibilities

- **Oversee extended school service provision within the school.**
- **Lead and manage the extended school provision on a daily basis.**
- **Undertake a comprehensive initial audit and assessment of current extended school activities and service provision, updating this annually, to identify, plan and map provision.**
- **Establish and maintain a database of extended school provision, keep records and collect registers.**
- **Consult with all relevant parties in the school and the local community, including pupils, parents, staff, governors and other relevant partners on extended school service provision.**
- **Devise and implement an extended school action plan in response to the findings from the comprehensive needs analysis (audit) and consultation process and report on its implementation.**
- **Market and promote the benefits of extended schooling.**
- **Manage the effective deployment of the extended school budget, including seeking additional further funding to support the implementation and development of existing and new extended school services, reporting on its usage.**
- **Liaise and work closely with senior managers in the school, the out-of-school-hours learning co-ordinator, the gifted and talented co-ordinator, the ethnic minority achievement co-ordinator, the inclusion co-ordinator, the SEN co-ordinator, the behaviour support co-ordinator and the leading teacher for pupil well-being.**

- **Liaise and work closely with all relevant external agencies and providers necessary for extended service delivery and establish a multi-agency partnership group who meet regularly to support the ongoing development of provision.**
- **Ensure health and safety legislation is observed and procedures for risk assessment are undertaken.**
- **Keep abreast of national and local extended school developments, disseminating information to school staff and service providers and other partners, where appropriate.**
- **Monitor, review and evaluate the effectiveness and impact of the extended school provision on pupils' attainment and well-being, reporting to the governing body, the senior leadership team and to other relevant interest groups.**
- **Support external providers, volunteers and parents and other staff running extended school activities and services.**
- **Act as a first point of contact in relation to any extended school queries from within or outside school.**
- **Participate in staff development and in-service training opportunities.**
- **Attend relevant local authority extended school co-ordinators' network and cluster group meetings.**
- **Ensure opportunities for celebrating and acknowledging the achievements of pupils and parents in extended school activities are recognised within the school's rewards and incentives scheme, and hold showcase events to publicise success in the local community.**

Person specification – Extended School Co-ordinator

Education and training

- **Degree or equivalent relevant professional/post-graduate qualifications associated with social services, health, education.**
- **High level of literacy, numeracy and proficient ICT skills.**
- **Evidence of continued professional development over the past two years.**
- **Evidence of further study or training in areas of management, community work, social care, health or education.**

Experience

- **Some experience of project management and/or securing external funding.**
- **Evidence of successful working within a multi-agency context, ideally with partners from the statutory, voluntary and private sectors.**
- **Awareness of the role of the school as a community resource in relation to extended schooling, lifelong learning, educational and social inclusion.**

Knowledge, skills and understanding

- **Knowledge and understanding of current issues affecting schools and communities.**
- **Knowledge and understanding of the role of different agencies/service providers.**
- **Knowledge of the National Service Framework, the *Every Child Matters* Outcomes Framework, the Common Assessment Framework and the OFSTED framework for the inspection of integrated children's services and extended school provision.**
- **Understanding of equal opportunities, disability legislation and an appreciation of cultural diversity.**
- **Understanding of the importance of health and safety in the workplace.**
- **Proven ability to work with, establish and maintain good relations between different service providers, partners and clients involved in extended school provision.**
- **Ability to develop, sustain and seek a range of partners as providers, through brokering and commissioning services.**
- **Proven ability to plan, organise and co-ordinate resources, evaluating performance outcomes against the extended school action plan.**
- **Ability to manage budgets and produce comprehensive best value financial reports on expenditure outcomes.**
- **Ability to advise, support and encourage parents, volunteers and local community members to assist in extended school service provision.**
- **Ability to motivate, encourage and inspire others.**
- **Ability to work independently, use initiative and work collaboratively with others.**
- **Ability to oversee the work of others who you line manage.**
- **Ability to organise and deliver briefings, information exchanges and training to a range of audiences.**

- **Ability to continue learning, undergo relevant training, taking responsibility for own continuing professional development.**
- **Ability to prioritise workload, manage own time effectively and delegate appropriately.**
- **Willingness to attend activities which occur outside working hours, e.g. weekends and during school holidays.**

Personal qualities

- **Excellent organisational skills.**
- **Exemplary health, attendance and punctuality record.**
- **Reliability and integrity.**
- **Enthusiasm.**
- **Innovative, creative and open-minded.**
- **Flexible, adaptable, problem solver.**
- **Effective communicator – verbally and non-verbally in writing.**
- **Has high standards and expectations of self and others.**
- **A good sense of humour.**
- **Commitment to inclusive education.**
- **Effective negotiator and facilitator.**
- **Emotionally intelligent.**
- **Diplomatic.**

There may be other key staff within the school, who participate in the delivery of extended school activities. If this is the case, it is important that their job descriptions reflect this aspect of their work. For example, the special educational needs co-ordinator (SENCO) is part of the school's overall extended school provision.

A team approach to managing extended school provision

A range of different management group structures exist. The most effective ones are briefly outlined in Table 6.1.

Table 6.1 Management structures in extended schools

Extended school working group	**Extended school project board**	**Extended school service team**	**Parent's action community team**
▪ Plan, review and evaluate extended school provision ▪ Membership: extended school co-ordinator, headteacher, governor, representative from partner schools, multi-agencies, local community ▪ Clearly defined terms of reference ▪ Supported by small sub-committees taking responsibility for different activity strands	▪ Ensures extended school operates within the LA strategy ▪ Ensures business plan focuses on DfES targets and objectives for extended schools ▪ Membership: representative from the LA and multi-agencies, together with parents, voluntary sector and local community ▪ Responsible for appointing additional staff ▪ Monitoring the performance of all service providers	▪ Adopt a solution-focused problem-solving approach to support extended school decision making ▪ Membership: (the same as the extended school working group) ▪ Develop, review and monitor the school's extended services ▪ Consultation with School Council ▪ Surveying what parents and families want in this service provision	▪ Acts as a community reference group ▪ Ensures local services are accessible ▪ Helps to co-ordinate local services ▪ Critiques the work of the extended school activities and services ▪ Provides valuable intelligence about the views and needs of the community ▪ Supports the extended school community development worker in helping to build relationships locally

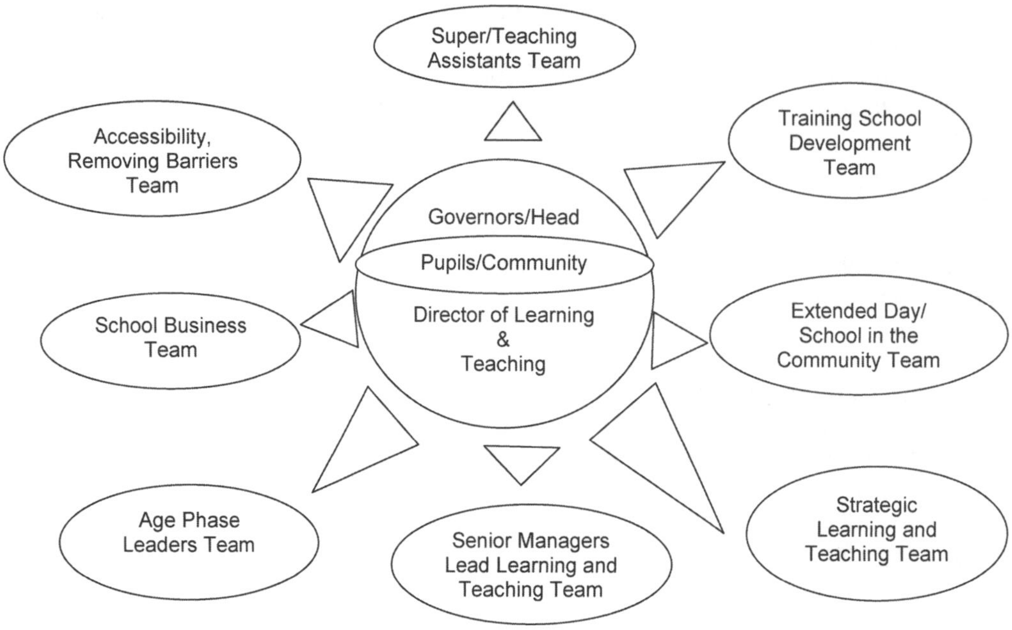

Figure 6.1 Example of managing the extended school. Source: Piper, J. (2005) *From Cutty Sark to Airbus – the Potential for extended Schools and their Communities.* PowerPoint presentation. London: The Extended Schools Support Service/ContinYou.

The structure in Figure 6.1 promotes:

- flexibility
- focused school work on key levers for improvement
- shared responsibilities
- innovation
- shared responsibility across a wider group
- information flow between all groups
- links and partnerships between agencies and other schools
- enhanced sharing of wider methodology

– Teams are identified (outer ovals)
– Central Strategic Team (inner circle)
– Leaders and managers of the outer ovals are strategic managers in their own field of responsibility and expertise, but acting as operational managers, they advise and feed this into the central strategic team, on a needs basis
– The operational managers ensure that decisions are actioned

Terms of reference for the Extended School Working Group

- **We will focus on organising and targeting services around the needs of children, parents, families and the local community.**
- **We will ensure that all services and activities provided are inclusive, accessible and meet the *Every Child Matters* outcomes.**
- **We will provide joined-up, well-co-ordinated wrap-around care and personalised services to support children and their families in the community.**
- **We will provide an appropriate range of enriching, interesting, relevant, barrier-free, out-of-school-hours, personalised learning activities and opportunities.**
- **We will consult with and listen to the views of children, young people, their families and the community in order to ensure their involvement in decisions about appropriate extended school provision.**
- **We will utilise best-value principles when procuring high-quality extended services.**
- **We will observe the principle that every child and everyone matters in this school and in the local community.**

Local authority support to extended schools

The support of the LA is crucial in locking the work of schools into wider strategies. A number of LA staff can help. These include the extended school remodelling adviser who may be a seconded head, an extended school strategic manager and one or two extended school LA co-ordinators who may have a specific focused brief for an aspect of extended school developments. Their roles are outlined in Table 6.2.

Table 6.2 Local authority support for extended schools

Extended school remodelling adviser	Extended school strategic manager	Extended school co-ordinator
▪ Provide support to schools on how to develop provision and help to make links with children's centres and other agencies ▪ Help to shape schools' understanding of extended school provision ▪ Support the school's monitoring and evaluation process of extended school provision ▪ Support school leaders with workforce remodelling to support developments in the initiative and *Every Child Matters.* ▪ Advise about how to use funding ▪ Provide advice on health and safety ▪ Advise on consultation with stakeholders ▪ Advise on and provide model policies for charging for services ▪ Advise on working with third-party providers and model contracts ▪ Provide training on aspects of extended schools	▪ Producing guidance for schools ▪ Developing and implementing LA extended school policy ▪ Producing agreed procedures and protocols for commissioning and accessing services ▪ Make explicit the roles of multi-agency services Children's Workforce ▪ Manage and allocate Standards Fund budget for extended school developments ▪ Implement and monitor LA extended school development plan ▪ Monitor and evaluate progress towards meeting the priorities on the LA extended school development plan ▪ Reporting to elected members, the Director of Children's Services and other relevant groups on extended school initiative	▪ Identify and disseminate best practice ▪ Audit and map extended school services ▪ Monitor schools ongoing work ▪ Provide advice, support, training and guidance direct to schools and to clusters on how to develop extended provision ▪ Facilitate and co-ordinate, LA extended schools network meetings ▪ Support local projects or trailblazer initiatives ▪ Develop effective working relationships with relevant services and agencies to the implementation of core offer ▪ Provide reports to the Children's Trust ▪ Keep school staff, governing bodies up to date with national and local developments related to the *Every Child Matters* and extended school agendas

How to manage the change process in extended schools

Use the checklist below to guide you through the process of change with staff.

Checklist for managing change in the extended school

- ❑ **Share the moral purpose – *Every Child Matters* outcomes make change necessary and shape the vision and mission statement.**
- ❑ **Help others understand the change process – share the big picture and promote working in new and different ways, avoiding initiative overload.**
- ❑ **Adopt a team approach, building trust between partners from within and outside the school.**
- ❑ **Re-design jobs and roles for staff in the school, to maximise upon their strengths in supporting extended school activities.**

- ❑ **Demonstrate emotional intelligence through sensitivity of needs of others. Look for new partnerships to build capacity.**
- ❑ **Develop more flexible organisational structures responsive to the needs of pupils and their parents/carers.**
- ❑ **Develop a learning culture and a learning community where participants learn from others, within and outside the school.**
- ❑ **Achieve coherence and connectedness – avoid taking too much on at once. Foster a solution-focused approach, whole school.**
- ❑ **Adopt the wider view to become an outward facing school:**
  - **relationships rather than individuals. The role of the extended school is to help pupils learn best with significant trusting adults at school, at home and in the community.**
  - **capacity building among staff to become less reliant on school leaders**
  - **make a difference locally by a shared local commitment, i.e. *'everyone matters in this community'*.**

Extended school leaders and the community role

Community engagement should be a top priority for every extended school leader. One young person, Lisa commented on community engagement:

> I like the idea of schools being more open and being used by the wider community. I think the youth and the rest of the community are separated and need to be more involved and know what is going on. This applies to the community knowing about what the school is doing and the school's knowing about what is going on in the community.
>
> (DfES 2004d: 8)

The National Standards for Headteachers (2004) make explicit the need for school leaders to assume a greater community role.

Use the following checklist as a point of reference for how to strengthen partnership with the community.

Headteachers strengthening the community

Knowledge

Knows about:

- ❑ **Current issues and future trends that impact on the school community**
- ❑ **The rich and diverse resources within local communities – both human and physical**
- ❑ **The wider curriculum beyond school and the opportunities it provides for pupils and the school community**
- ❑ **Models of school, home, community and business partnerships**
- ❑ **The work of other agencies and opportunities for collaboration**
- ❑ **Strategies which encourage parents and carers to support their children's learning**
- ❑ **The strengths, capabilities and objectives of other schools**

Professional qualities

Is committed to:

- ❑ **Effective team work within the school and with extended partners;**
- ❑ **Working with other agencies for the well-being of all pupils and their families;**
- ❑ **Involvement of parents and the community in supporting the learning of children and in defining and realising the school vision;**
- ❑ **Collaboration and networking with other schools to improve outcomes**

Is able to:

- ❑ **Recognise and take account of the richness and diversity of the school's communities;**
- ❑ **Engage in a dialogue which builds partnerships and community consensus on values, beliefs and shared responsibilities;**

- ❑ **Listen to, reflect and act on community feedback;**
- ❑ **Build and maintain effective relationships with parents, carers, partners and the community that enhance the education of all pupils**

Actions

- ❑ **Builds on school culture and curriculum which takes account of the richness and diversity of the school's communities**
- ❑ **Creates and promotes positive strategies for challenging racial and other prejudice and dealing with racial harassment**
- ❑ **Ensures learning experiences for pupils are linked into and integrated with the wider community**
- ❑ **Ensures a range of community-based learning experiences**
- ❑ **Collaborates with other agencies in providing for the academic, spiritual, moral, social, emotional and cultural well-being of pupils and their families**
- ❑ **Creates and maintains an effective partnership with parents and carers to support and improve pupils' achievement and personal development**
- ❑ **Seeks opportunities to invite parents and carers, community figures, businesses or other organisations into the school to enhance and enrich the school and its values to the wider community**
- ❑ **Contributes to the development of the education system by, for example, sharing effective practice, working in partnership with other schools and promoting innovative initiatives**
- ❑ **Co-operates and works with relevant agencies to protect children.**

(DfES 2004e: 11)

Leaders of extended schools need to do things with the community as equal partners, finding out what the community wants in the extended school provision. The deputy headteacher of an inner city primary school in an excellence cluster commented:

> It's not up to us to patronise our parents by telling them what help they need. They have their own ideas about what the school should do for them. . . . We have established a weekly 'pop-in' half hour session where parents who are available can come and talk to us about how they feel their children are getting on and what help they feel we might arrange for them. Once a month we arrange the session in the evening just before the Sure Start Centre closes at 6.00p.m. so that parents who are not free during the day can come and talk to us.
>
> (OFSTED 2006b: 14)

Consultation

Why consult and who with?

The Education Act 2002 requires governing bodies of schools to consult with registered pupils, their parents/carers, families, the wider community, staff and the LA, including with other schools and those from statutory, private, voluntary and community organisations, who will develop and run extended services for a defined community.

Ongoing consultation with stakeholders enables extended schools and children's centres to:

- identify and assess the services and activities required to meet local needs, and audit existing services;
- identify resources required, e.g. time, people, money;
- alert service providers and partners to the extended services and activities required, involving them in planning and developing provision;
- engage and involve members of the wider community in the development of extended service provision;
- publicise extended service proposals to the local community;
- respond to changing local circumstances by adapting services to meet new requirements.

Consultation will be influenced by factors such as the type of school, its location and situation and the nature of the surrounding community.

When to consult

Consultation should occur at the earliest opportunity, and a clear consultation plan needs to be developed which indicates:

- the timescale for consultation;
- the resources required to support the consultation process;
- which stakeholders, and at what stage they will be requested to contribute to the consultation
- a clear communications plan;
- the consultation methods and materials required;
- evaluation of the outcomes from consultation;
- feedback to stakeholders on the outcomes from consultation.

How to consult

A range of methods can be utilised during the consultation process about extended service provision. These include:

- **focus groups** – collecting information and views on a predetermined set of discussion topics from six to eight representatives from a cross-section of the community;
- **questionnaires and surveys** – distributed to members of the community;
- **community meetings** – and the facility for those not able to attend such meetings to respond via a consultation website, by telephone or through a local community leader;
- **Evaluation forms** – given to current service users
- **Constant listening** – in formal and informal situations to the parents and carers, pupils and other users through the Parent Teacher Association (PTA), Parents or Community Forums, Pupil Councils
- **Networking with other organisations** – i.e. Sure Start, Connexions, local Learning and Skills Council, other schools, community-based clubs, societies, faith and youth organisations, LA, Primary Case Trust (PCT), police, regeneration groups.

Cameo of school utilising a community conversation strategy

The headteacher of a primary school in Keighley held a 'community conversation' on the same day as the school had an in-service training day. The purpose of the conversation was to bring together all the people and groups whose life and work impacted on children on the school's roll. Those attending included: parents, school staff, community and religious leaders, health, social services, police, Sure Start, LA, voluntary groups, representatives operational, strategic, managerial and officer levels.

The central aim of the community conversation day was to enable all the participants to gain a deeper understanding of the roles of others in the lives of the children, to ascertain what their aspirations and targets for the future might be and how groups could work together to enable all those involved to fulfil them.

A neutral facilitator was utilised to lead the community conversation. The day was action-focused, with specific tasks that had high impact, were easy to implement and gave quick wins, as well as more challenging tasks. Sufficient time was provided for networking opportunities during the day. Terminology was clarified as well as the protocols for information sharing and inter-agency working and communication. Overall the exercise helped to build social capital in the community, and to create a better understanding of the environment that children as learners are living and working in.

Further information about the approach described in the cameo can be found on the National College for School Leadership (NCSL) website: www.ncsl.org.uk/researchpublications

The publication is entitled *Community Conversation. Developing Extended Schools through Stakeholder Consultation* (NCSL 2006e).

Outcomes following consultation

Constructive feedback on the outcomes of consultation needs to indicate any changes to be made in service provision, and the reasons why some service expectations cannot currently be met. The analysis of all the consultation information will enable proposals to be developed and informed decision making to take place. The process will include focused discussions on:

- how extended services and activities will be resourced;
- who will co-ordinate and run them;
- when the services and activities will be available, e.g. daytime, evenings, weekends, in the holidays;
- how much to charge for particular services and activities.

Following discussion a development plan will need to be formulated. This will be responsive and flexible to the evolving community needs.

Consultation with pupils, parents and the community about extended provision must continue once services have been established.

Further information about consultation can be found on the following website:

- www.teachernet.gov.uk/wholeschool/extendedschools/practicalknowhow. The Contin You/ DfES leaflet/entitled *Consultation.* can be downloaded from the teachernet website:
- www.dfes.gov.uk/listeningtolearn. The publication entitled: *Building a Culture of Participation* can be downloaded from the DfES website, which focuses on involving children and young people in consultation.
- www.nya.org.uk. The National Youth Agency website has a useful publication that can be downloaded, entitled: *Putting Young People at the Centre of the Extended School.*

What extended services should the school provide?

A valuable source of information about your local community can be found by accessing the neighbourhood statistics website: www.neighbourhood.statistics.gov.uk

Once the home page appears on the screen, type in your school/children's centre post code and press 'enter'. You will obtain a full Neighbourhood Profile. This data will provide an insight into key aspects and issues of community life, population and demographic features in your area. This information can be used to help prioritise the appropriate extended school services and activities to meet local needs.

A useful activity to undertake with key stakeholders, e.g. staff, governors and service providers, is to produce some school locality data headlines. This will help to raise stakeholder awareness and put the provision of extended school services in context.

COMMUNITY SURVEY FOR LEADERS AND MANAGERS

Using the data and information from the local neighbourhood statistics, complete the following survey, to help you plan for extended services and activities.

1. **How would you describe the nature of your community?**

   rural urban suburban mixture

2. **What particular local community issues have you identified in relation to:**

   (a) **economic activity** – unemployment, employment schemes like 'New Deal'

   (b) **crime and safety** – youth offending

   (c) **education, skills and training** – children, students, adults

   (d) **health and care** – at risk factors; mental health, teenage pregnancies, alcohol/drug misuse

   (e) **housing and households** – transience, homelessness, travellers

   (f) **people and society** – population trends: age profiles, ethnicity, one parent families, teenage mothers, deprivation, domestic violence

3. **What community and voluntary organisations/programmes already exist to support children and families experiencing difficulties?**

4. **What barriers exist that inhibit community access to extended school provision?**

   e.g. isolated rural communities, poor public transport, low incomes, lack of childcare

5. **From the evidence gathered, what extended activities and services will you prioritise in this year's programme of school/centre activities?**

Figure 6.2 Community survey for leaders and managers

Illustrated below is an example of local community headline data, and how this can be used with staff and other interested parties to plan provision.

Maple School Local Community Headlines Data

During the month of July in this school's locality there were:

- **30 babies born**
- **5 of those babies born were to teenage mothers**
- **15 children and young people were reported to the local Safeguarding Board as having experienced child abuse**
- **20 children and young people were permanently excluded from neighbouring schools within the cluster, which included 2 children from our own school**
- **8 incidents of juvenile crime were reported by the police and the Youth Offending Team**
- **12 incidents of teenage substance and drug misuse were reported, of which 3 were children and young people from our school**

Overall, in the local community:

- **21% of 16–74 year olds have no formal qualifications**
- **5% of the local population aged 16–74 are unemployed, as a result of the recent closure of a local factory**
- **2% of the local population aged 16–74 are registered disabled**

Follow up activities

1. In view of this local information, what extended school services should we realistically be providing to meet the identified needs of the community?
2. Do members of the local community, including parents, fully agree with the extended services we have highlighted as needing to be provided?
3. What additional extended school services and activities may be required?
4. Is it realistically possible to provide all the identified extended school services on the current levels of funding and staffing available?
5. How can we work together with other local schools and the children's centre in the locality to ensure there is no duplication or gap in service provision?

Role of the extended school governing body

The four prime key roles of the governing body in relation to extended school services are:

- ongoing monitoring, evaluation and overseeing of the extended activities, usually as part of a steering group;
- helping to locate supplementary funding sources for extended school initiatives;
- safeguarding the delegated budget for extended school provision;
- securing suitable insurance and appointing extra staff to support and manage the initiative.

Section 27 of the Education Act 2002 gives governing bodies of all maintained schools the enabling power to provide, or enter into contract to provide, facilities and services that 'further any charitable purpose for the benefit of pupils at the school, their families or people who live or work in the locality in which the school is situated'. Charitable purposes are defined as:

- the relief of financial hardship;
- the advancement of education;
- the advancement of religion and certain other purposes for the benefit of the community.

Section 28 of the Education Act 2002 puts a statutory duty and requirement on governing bodies to consult widely before establishing and providing extended services. They must, as a minimum, consult parents of children registered at the school, the children (where appropriate), staff and the local authority, and with workplace unions, as well as with others the governing body considers appropriate, e.g. Primary Care Trusts, local businesses, voluntary organisations.

The governing body of a school controls the use of the school premises, both during and outside school hours. Governing bodies cannot provide any service that might interfere with their main duty to educate pupils, or their responsibility to promote high standards of educational achievement at the school.

The governing body is required to set up procedures for dealing with all complaints relating to its extended school activities and the facilities and services provided directly by the school, and to publicise the procedures to all users.

The governing body should ensure that any third party providers offering activities and services through the school premises, or using school facilities, have their own complaints procedures in place.

Below you will find two useful checklists for the governors:

(1) Tips for governors to consider in developing extended school services;
(2) Extended schools governance checklist.

Tips for governors to consider in developing extended school services

- **Set up a steering group/committee of key stakeholders to oversee, and be accountable for, the development of extended services.**
- **Agree a vision. Plan and focus services so that they can contribute to supporting school improvement and to supporting pupils, their families and communities.**
- **Talk to other local providers of children's services – health professionals, social services, voluntary sector – for opportunities to work together.**
- **Get to know the community. Audit existing services and consult pupils, families, school staff and the wider community.**
- **Look to what local groups and individuals in the community can offer in the way of skills to contribute to extended school development.**
- **Decide what the school can realistically offer.**
- **Get teachers and other school staff on board from the beginning.**
- **Seek someone to take on responsibility for the day-to-day management of the extended services to avoid overloading staff with additional responsibilities.**
- **Speak to other schools in the area to see if you can cluster and share extended services provision across settings, and seek advice.**
- **Think about how you can make best use of the funding you have already got, and how other services may contribute.**

Extended schools governance checklist

(✓ The relevant box when you have undertaken each activity.)

- ❑ **You have checked which governance model fits best with your school's development and vision for extended school services.**
- ❑ **You have a system in place to develop the right governance structure for an extended school.**
- ❑ **You have sought advice from, and discussed your extended school governance with, the local authority governor services.**
- ❑ **You have considered the legal implications and liabilities for governors, the headteacher and any other group involved in the extended school initiative.**
- ❑ **You feel confident that your present governance structure is the right one to lead an extended school.**
- ❑ **You have explored the recruitment of more governors with the necessary skills and expertise in extended schooling from various agencies of the services (health and social care) and from voluntary, community and private sector organisations.**

- ❑ **Your governing body does reflect the community and the future extended school provision.**
- ❑ **You have a recruitment process in place.**
- ❑ **Your governing body reflects the involvement of other agencies and organisations.**
- ❑ **You have reviewed your committee structure to reflect a wider responsibility and accountability for extended school service provision**
- ❑ **You have ensured that there are opportunities for parental groups to give feedback to the governing body.**
- ❑ **You have given consideration to working with another school's governing body to provide an accountability structure.**
- ❑ **You have built in reporting procedures to be kept aware of extended school services progress, especially if your governing body is not leading the development of your extended services.**
- ❑ **You have given consideration as to how the governing body is going to monitor and provide feedback on the impact of extended services.**

(Adapted from NRT 2006: 15)

Further detailed information about governance in extended schools can be found at: www.governornet.co.uk and in the National Remodelling Team (NRT) publication entitled *Extended Schools – a Guide for Governors 1.*

The role of the Head of a children's centre

A range of titles exists in relation to this important position, e.g. Centre Director, Head of Centre, Centre Co-ordinator and Centre Manager. Head of Centre is the preferred option, however, irrespective of the title, they need to think globally and be community activists.

The head of centre establishes ground rules around flexibility, honesty and mutual respect for the different professionals working in the children's centre, helping to establish a baseline for professional terms and conditions.

Large children's centres find it beneficial to have a Deputy Head of Centre to share the increasing workload with the manager. It is also valuable to appoint a Team Co-ordinator to oversee delivery staff from all external services in order to support and guide them, while working in the children's centre.

The following job description and person specification provide a suggested model, which can be customised and adapted to suit the particular context of the children's centre.

JOB DESCRIPTION

Job title: Head of Children's Centre
Grade: PM2
Hours: Full-time
Location: Maple Children's Centre
Responsible to: Sure Start Manager
Job purpose: Contribute to the development and delivery of integrated services for children and families in the local area
Co-ordinate and manage service delivery to meet identified local needs
Manage the children's centre effectively through joint working with stakeholders.

Main duties and responsibilities

- **In accordance with the Children Act 2004, take a lead in ensuring the needs of children and families are identified early and met through the provision of appropriate integrated services and wrap-around care**
- **Manage, administer and organise service provision from the children's centre to meet the *Every Child Matters* outcomes framework, the National Standards Framework; and other relevant national strategies**
- **Quality assure service provision from the children's centre**

- **Ensure the effective and efficient deployment of allocated budgets and resources within the children's centre**
- **Produce a children's centre service delivery plan that reflects and responds to local needs, statutory requirements and local authority policies**
- **Oversee the maintenance of the children's centre and its facilities**
- **Implement appropriate governance structures and procedures that foster the involvement of key stakeholders, which are inclusive and reflect local diversity**
- **Promote appropriate parent/carer involvement in the work of the children's centre, and establish good links with local partners**
- **Raise expectations and aspirations of families and the local community**
- **Oversee and manage the recruitment, induction and development of staff working within the children's centre**
- **Maintain appropriate records; collect and analyse data; monitor and evaluate the effectiveness and impact of service provision**
- **Prepare reports for a range of audiences to demonstrate and measure successful outcomes**
- **Ensure that appropriate assessment, referral and allocation systems are in place, which support the Common Assessment Framework process and conform to the Safeguarding Children Regulations**
- **Promote and support the continuous professional development of staff (including self), through the implementation of appraisal and supervision**
- **Liaise and work collaboratively with professionals from multi-agencies, including private and voluntary sector colleagues, in order to provide well co-ordinated and coherent services that meet the needs of the whole child and their family**
- **Promote and maintain high quality, appropriate learning environments for young children that meet their personal, social and intellectual development needs**
- **Ensure safeguarding, health and safety, equal opportunities and customer care policy and procedures are followed by all staff working within the centre**
- **Participate in and attend relevant children's centre national, regional and local conferences, forums and network meetings**
- **Keep abreast of national and local children's centre developments, disseminating information to centre staff, service providers and other relevant partners**
- **Ensure opportunities for publicising, celebrating and acknowledging the achievements of the children's centre are recognised through holding showcase events, open days and other activities**
- **Undertake other duties commensurate with the post, as allocated by the Sure Start Manager**

PERSON SPECIFICATION – HEAD OF CHILDREN'S CENTRE

Education and training

- **Relevant childcare, education, social work or health qualification at graduate level**
- **Willingness to undertake the National Professional Qualification for Integrated Centre Leadership (NPQICL)**
- **Evidence of relevant continued professional development over the past two years**

Experiences

Evidence of:

- **developing and managing services in an early years and/or family support setting;**
- **successful consultation and partnership working with a range of stakeholders and partners from statutory, voluntary and private sectors to plan and deliver integrated services to children and families**
- **commissioning, brokering and procuring services**
- **successful budget management and securing external funding**
- **supervising and managing staff effectively**
- **monitoring, reviewing and evaluating service delivery and provision against national standards**
- **some previous experience of project management**

Knowledge, skills and understanding

- **Secure knowledge and understanding of the Early Years Foundation Stage curriculum framework, the Ten Year Strategy for Childcare and the Five Year Strategy for Children and Learners**
- **Knowledge and understanding of what constitutes effective observation, learning, teaching and assessment**

- **Knowledge and understanding of *Every Child Matters*, the National Service Framework, the Common Assessment Framework and the OFSTED framework for the inspection of integrated children's services**
- **Ability to manage services within a complex framework of governance that reflect and respect the diversity and needs of the local community**
- **Ability to think analytically and use initiative**
- **Ability to make sound professional judgements based on secure evidence**
- **Ability to work under pressure, deal with competing priorities, manage self and prioritise workload**
- **Ability to manage any potential conflict and maintain effective working relationships at all levels**
- **Ability to utilise and promote ICT within the children's centre in order to increase effective service administration and delivery**
- **Ability to communicate effectively with a wide range of audiences in written and non-written formats, producing clear and concise reports**
- **Ability to collect, analyse and interpret information and data**
- **Ability to deal with the unexpected and work to deadlines**

Personal qualities

- **Commitment to inclusion, equal opportunities and cultural diversity**
- **Enthusiastic advocate of holistic, integrated service provision in a children's centre**
- **Effective communicator, negotiator, mediator and facilitator**
- **Diplomatic, politically astute and sensitive to the needs of others**
- **Flexible, adaptable and well organised**
- **Willingness to undertake continuous professional development**
- **Inspire and motivate others**
- **Approachable**
- **Reflective practitioner**
- **Fosters mutual trust and respect**
- **Values the contributions and views of others**
- **Good sense of humour**

The National Standards for the head of a Children's Centre are closely aligned to the key areas of responsibility identified in the National Standards for Headteachers, published in October 2004.

Table 6.3 National Standards for headteachers and heads of children's centres

National Standards for Headteachers – Key Areas	National Standards for Heads of Children's Centres – Key Areas
■ Shaping the future ■ Leading learning and Teaching ■ Developing Self and Working with others ■ Managing the organisation ■ Securing Accountability ■ Strengthening the Community	■ Shaping the present and Creating the future ■ Leading learning and development ■ Building and strengthening Teams ■ Managing the organisation ■ Being accountable and responsible ■ Stronger families, Stronger communities

The National Standards reflect the challenge and complexity of the role of Head of Centre in relation to creating integrated, accessible and comprehensive services for children and families that contribute to improving children's physical and mental health, their learning and achievement.

The purpose of the National Standards for Leaders of Integrated Centres for Children and Families is to:

- specify the qualities, skills and understanding required;
- exemplify current best practice;
- exemplify future extension and improvement;

- assess the leadership capability of participants completing the NCSL training;
- inform job descriptions, person specifications and performance management.

The Head of Centre is the government's preferred terminology for this post.

The role of the teacher in children's centres

The government's Ten Year Strategy for Childcare (HM Treasury 2004) emphasised the importance of any full-time day-care setting, which includes children's centres, being led by a graduate-qualified early years professional (a pedagogue).

Having a qualified teacher in a children's centre brings many benefits:

- the status of the provision in the children's centre is raised;
- a teacher is able to provide seamless integrated early education and care;
- placements can be provided for trainee early years and primary teachers;
- a holistic approach to meeting the needs of children is adopted;
- a teacher brings a wealth of experience to staff working in nurseries;
- it is easier to liaise and link up with multi-agency professionals working in the children's centre to plan specific programmes for young children with additional needs;
- a teacher helps to support the smoother transfer from children's centre to primary school.

The *Effective Provision of Pre-School Education* research (Sylva *et al.* 2004) indicated that where a qualified teacher leads in planning, developing and delivering the early years curriculum, the quality of provision is good and there are improved outcomes for children.

A part-time equivalent early years teacher based in every children's centre is a minimum requirement. It is recommended that a full-time qualified early years teacher is employed over the first 18 months that the children's centre is in operation.

Teachers working in a children's centre will be expected to have the following knowledge and skills:

- specialist knowledge of working with young children and leading early years settings;
- an understanding of the roles and responsibilities of other professionals working in the children's centre (and linked settings);
- an ability to establish effective professional relationships with all colleagues from a range of backgrounds and services, respecting their expertise and knowledge, e.g. midwives, health visitors, speech and language therapists, family support workers, community play workers;
- a commitment to developing self and other colleagues as learners, acting as a mentor and role model to other children's centre staff;
- the ability to lead a team of key workers, including the training and support of childminders;
- a substantial input into planning the integrated day, and designing age-appropriate play and learning activities;
- the ability to promote family and intergenerational learning by running parents groups on various aspects to enable them to support their child's learning at home;
- the ability to co-ordinate an area of learning or an aspect of the Foundation Stage curriculum across age groups;
- the ability to lead curriculum projects across the children's centre;
- the ability to support pre-school and birth-to-three staff;
- the ability to plan and supervise students on placements;
- the ability to quality assure early learning provision through robust monitoring, self-evaluation of outcomes for children.

One LA employs pedagogues (qualified early years teachers) on Soulbury 1–4 offering 25–30 days annual leave. In most children's centres teachers are employed or seconded on standard pay and conditions.

Key principles of successful children's centre management

DfES research (2005) to inform best practice in the successful management and governance of children's centres identifies the following key principles:

- **cohesive**, with a shared philosophy, shared vision and values;
- **unified**, with a single (operational) line management structure and ideally on a single site (with the exception of rural centres);
- **participative** in the approach to staff management, with effective channels of communication set up, utilising, in particular, regular team meetings;
- **trust-based**, allowing staff the freedom to work on initiative and to innovate;
- **accessible**, with an informal and supportive relationship between management and the frontline;
- **led decisively** by either the centre manager or a united and experienced governing body;
- **supportive** of the centre manager, enabling her/him to develop partnership working ability, leadership skills and the ability to engage communities, building in support roles where desired;
- **co-ordinated** in its approach to joint delivery with the role of the centre manager not being to line manage but to co-ordinate and align services for maximum impact;
- **standardised** in relation to staff terms and conditions, to secure buy-in and reduce potential conflict;
- **joined up** in delivery wherever possible, including joint training to foster co-operation and integration of the different professions.

(DfES/Sure Start 2005: x)

Table 6.4 School-based governance structures for children's centres

Children's centre governance fully integrated to school governing body	Children's centre governance partially integrated with school governing body	Children's centre governance parallel to school governing body
▪ Local authority acts as the accountable body but commissions the provision of the children's centre through the school. ▪ The responsibilities of the school's governing body are extended to include the functions and long term vision of the integrated children's centre. ▪ To ensure the school governing body can cope with the flexible demands of multi-agency working, additional capacity provided, i.e. through a sub-committee of the school board, or by the establishment of a parallel children's centre board consisting of representatives of the school governing body and school management board, local authority and strategic partners, and community representatives.	▪ Partially integrated governance arrangements between the school and the children's centre. ▪ An operational board is established consisting of school representatives, the head of children's centre, strategic support and an independent chair. ▪ This board oversees day-to-day management and co-exists with the children's centre board who are responsible for governance. ▪ The head of children's centre also sits on the school governing body. ▪ Management decisions are taken jointly between the school and local authority but the latter remain the accountable body.	▪ 'Hybrid' centres developed from a variety of settings and including a maintained nursery school. ▪ Maintain the maintained nursery school governing body in parallel to and separate from the governance arrangements of the children's centre as a whole.

Source: DfES/Sure Start (2005) *Research to Inform the Management and Governance of Children's Centres*. London: SQW Limited/ Department for Education and Skills.

Key principles of successful governance of children's centres

The following key principles were identified as underlying the successful governance arrangements of children's centres by the DfES in 2005.

- **Responsive** to community needs and able to take decisions rapidly to tackle the needs of disadvantaged communities – this includes effective monitoring and evaluation of services.
- **Clear** with respect to functions and roles.
- **Committed** to promoting a common vision and Sure Start values.
- **Robust** and sustainable to ensure continuity of quality service provision, with risk being formally and effectively managed.
- **Engaged** with parents to the fullest possible extent, ideally through significant parental representation on the management board or alternatively through parent forums.
- **Involved** with the wider community at a high level.
- **Structured** to promote partnership working and joint delivery.

(DfES/Sure Start 2005: 53)

Features of good governance in children's centres

The features listed below are essential to the good governance of children's centres:

- **focused on purpose and outcomes;**
- **clarity of functions, roles and responsibilities** – especially of executive and non-executive members;
- **promotion and demonstration of the values of the centre;**
- **informed and transparent decision making and risk management;**
- **development of capacity for effective governance** – a succession strategy and representatives from a range of services on the governing body, or on the management board;
- **engagement of stakeholders and real accountability** – including setting up a multi-agency committee as part of the governing body, to act as associate members or advisers.

Engaging parents in the governance of children's centres

Best practice in engaging parents is through the formation of a parent forum, a 'Friends' group or a parent network. These groups provide:

- valuable feedback to the governing body on what services should be delivered by the children's centre and how existing services could be improved;
- assistance in scoping the demand for planned services;
- feedback information to parents from the management board meetings;
- assistance with the usual fundraising and voluntary activities.

Strategies to successfully engage parents in governance

The following strategies have been successful in engaging parents in the governance of children's centres:

- family open days;
- social events such as a fun day or 'tea and toast';
- informal engagement during visits to the centre;
- posters advertising the parent forum, and monthly newsletters in a range of alternative formats and languages;
- Use of an information centre on the high street to market services;

- Flexible timing of parent forum and other meetings;
- Free crèche for parent forum and other meetings;
- Holding parent forum meetings in a community venue, away from the children's centre, on occasions;
- Establishing a position of family link worker or client service manager to provide outreach to communities and to facilitate parent forums and feedback information to the management board.

In relation to the governance of children's centres, one headteacher of a nursery and children's centre in West Sussex, commented:

> Governors are on a steep learning curve, particularly in terms of where their responsibilities begin and end. . . . My governing body is thinking, 'How on earth do we make this work?'
>
> (TES 2006)

The Chair of Governors from the same nursery and children's centre stated:

> We know what our role is with regard to the maintained nursery school. . . . When you go into the further reaches of involving the primary care trust and Jobcentre Plus and working collaboratively with other agencies, we are asking who we are relating to as a governing body, and what our role is.
>
> (ibid.)

Further activities for school leaders and heads of children's centres

The following questions are designed to enable you to discuss and identify the ways forward, in meeting the challenges and opportunities posed for leaders of extended schools and heads of children's centres.

- What additional capacity and management structures are required in order to provide the necessary services?
- How can the increased leadership and management demands arising from the development of extended services and wrap-around care be managed effectively?
- What do you know already about the local community and what it requires in the way of extended services and wrap-around care?
- What else do you need to find out about the community, and which data sources will you utilise to inform service provision and delivery?
- Are you secure about the legal position if services offered do not match up to users' expectations?
- How will you prevent the extended services and wrap-around care from being perceived by some families in the community as intruding and interfering in their lives?
- How will you balance the different styles and ways of working between teachers and frontline workers from multi-agencies?
- How will you ensure that charging for some services and activities does not disadvantage and reduce access for those families and children who do not have sufficient money to pay for them?

7

Quality Assurance

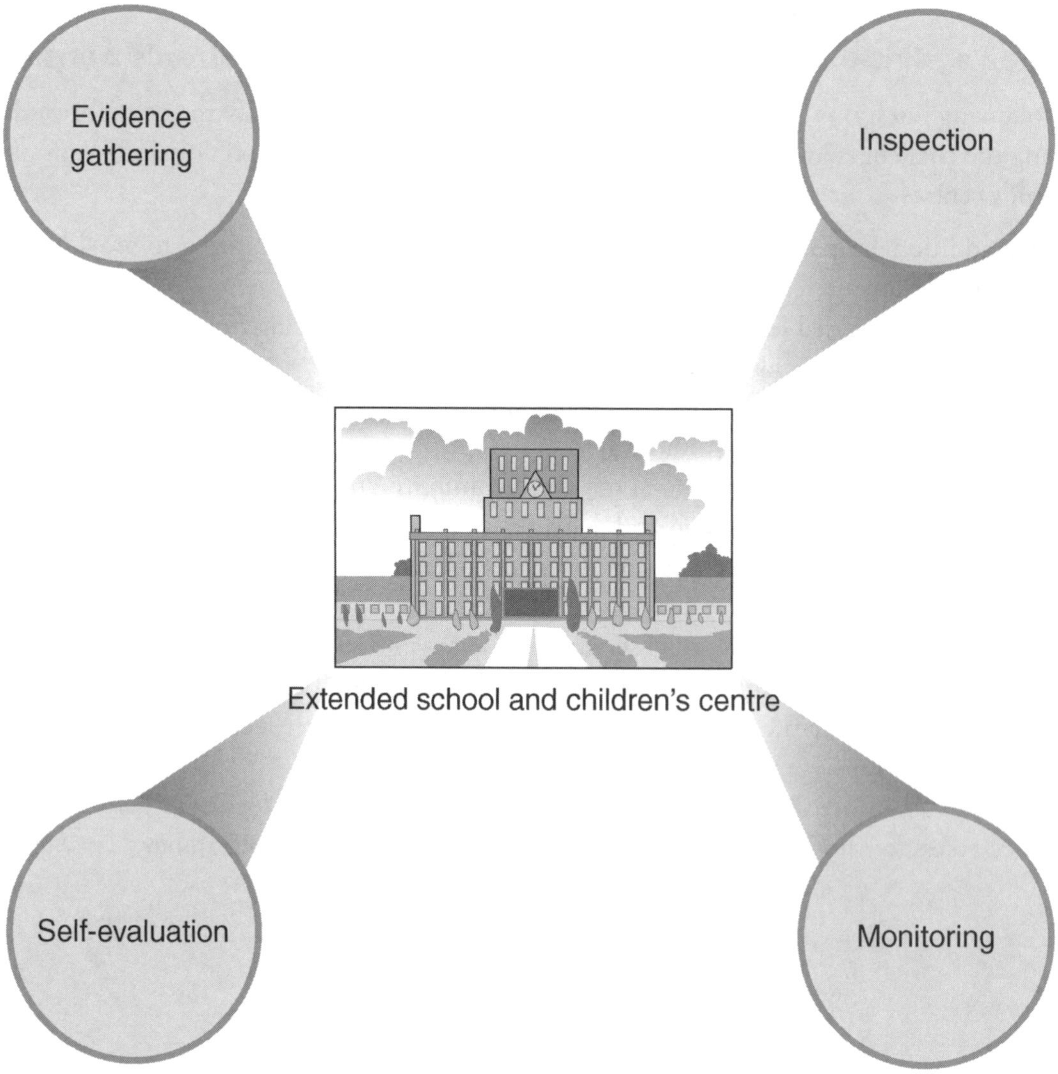

Key terminology

A key part of the quality assurance process is setting objectives and expected outcomes for the extended school and children's centre provision, and then collecting evidence to see whether the objectives and expected outcomes have been achieved. Schools and children's centres are judged on the extent to which they understand local needs and opinions, and how they act on these to improve provision for their clients within the community.

Monitoring and evaluation as an ongoing collaborative process engages a range of stakeholders and partners from within and outside the setting.

A useful starting point prior to undertaking the process of quality assurance is to clarify key terminology.

- **Performance** looks at what has happened as a result of the activities and services provided, and the effect of extended school activities and children's centre provision on individuals, the community and those providing the services.
- **Monitoring** is the activity of checking and recording ongoing progress against agreed objectives and targets. For example, keeping records of attendance and participation data to support the measuring of outcomes.
- **Evaluation** is the analysis of how well the extended school and children's centre provision have met their key objectives. Evaluation is also concerned with gauging overall effectiveness and identifying strengths and weaknesses in provision.
- **Qualitative evaluation** focuses on gathering evidence from stakeholders and other partners about their experiences, feelings and expectations in relation to extended school activities and children's centre provision.
- **Quantitative evaluation** is concerned with numerical and statistical evidence in relation to judging the outcomes of extended school and children's centre provision on clients.

ContinYou/DfES in their 'know how' guidance (2005e) confirm that evaluation is important to:

> - provide accurate baseline and contextual information at the beginning and end of year to assess the outcomes and improvement;
> - inform ongoing decision-making and assess whether an activity or service has achieved, or is on target to meet its aims and objectives;
> - show what has happened as a result of the extended school initiative or children's centre provision;
> - improve practice and inform future planning, strategy and development;
> - secure support – financial and in-kind for the extended school and children's centre initiative;
> - meet the requirement to present evidence to OfSTED and any other external body of the impact and outcomes of extended provision on children, young people, their families and the community.
>
> (ContinYou/DfES 2005e: 3)

The evaluation process is summarised in the following figure.

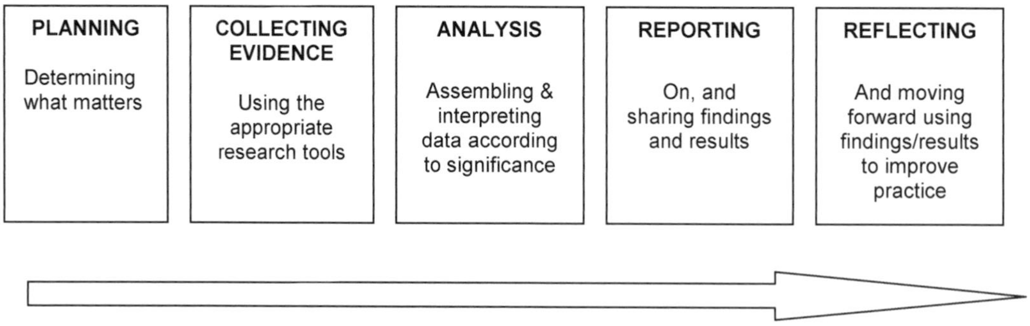

Figure 7.1 The evaluation process. Source: ContinYou/DfES (2005e) *Evidence and Evaluation.* London: ContinYou? Department of Education and Skills.

The purpose of monitoring

Any monitoring system used within the school or children's centre should:

- gather information from the start in order to provide baseline data;
- gather information in the same format over time, in order to make valid comparisons.

Information will need to be collected on:

- identifying any trends in provision;
- the needs of the children, young people, parents/carers, families and the community accessing the services;
- the outcomes for service users, i.e. the achievements of children, young people and for parents participating in adult learning, parenting classes, including 'real people' accounts as a measure of success;
- the views of service users about what they have received;
- the views of parents/carers about the extended provision their child has accessed;
- the views of other agencies, third-party service providers and school or children's centre staff directly delivering services.

While data from monitoring provides information for the evaluation of services, care must be taken when analysing improvements in this aspect, as such improvements in outcomes for children, young people, parents, community may not be attributed solely to extended provision.

The purpose of evaluation

Evaluation has two main related purposes:

1 To answer questions about the **impact** of services, initiatives and projects, including:
   - specific outcomes for service users;
   - impacts for different groups of users or organisations;
   - how and why services achieve or do not achieve their objectives.
2 To answer questions about the **processes**, **structures** and **outputs** in delivery and implementation of services, initiatives and projects, e.g.
   - what is delivered, to whom, and how;
   - what are the characteristics and needs of participants;
   - who is not being reached by the service, initiative or project;
   - what are the barriers and challenges in delivery;
   - what are best practice solutions and lessons learned.

Table 7.1 Extended school service provision recording log

Service description/ activities	**Service provider**	**Venue/ Location**	**Session length/ frequency**	**Funding source/ charge**	**Client group** (Age, gender, FSM, ethnicity)	**Nos attending** (Maximum, minimum, total numbers)	**Client satisfaction levels**	**Service quality, outcomes and viability**
CHILDCARE								
YOUTH SERVICES								
OUT-OF-HOURS LEARNING								
SPECIALIST SERVICES								
SUPPORT FOR PARENTS								
COMMUNITY USE								

Table 7.2 Children's centre service provision recording log

Service description	**Service provider**	**Room/ Location**	**Service session length, frequency**	**Target client group(s)**	**Nos attending** (Maximum, minimum, total)	**Funding source/charge**	**Client satisfaction levels**	**Service quality & outcomes**
EARLY YEARS PROVISION –Childcare –Education								
PARENTING AND FAMILY SUPPORT								
EDUCATION, TRAINING & EMPLOYMENT SERVICES								
HEALTH SERVICES								
SPECIALIST SERVICES – Speech & lang. therapy – Family therapy – Outreach/home visiting								

In reality, the long-term impact of extended school service provision is likely not to be evident for at least five years. In their HMI report on extended services, which was published in July 2006, OfSTED commented:

> Schools and children's centres find it difficult to measure the impact of the services: many interventions and developments were expected to provide considerable impact over time, but not in the short term.
>
> (OFSTED 2006c: 17).

It is also appropriate to consider the effect of extended school activity as part of the sum of the whole continuum of flexible provision for children and young people.

Evaluating the impact, benefits and difference that multi-agency/extended service providers make to the outcomes for children remains a challenge. The integration of the *Every Child Matters* Outcomes Framework with the the National Service Framework for Children, Young People and Maternity Services will enable school leaders and heads of children's centres to assess and evaluate collaborative activity from external service providers. This will help to establish the extent to which such outcomes can be attributed to partnership working, or otherwise. For example, would the outcome for children have occurred irrespective of the partnership?

Clearly, the added value of extended school service provision is evident in the ability of the school and multi-agency services in helping to address the issues of deprivation, and in caring for the whole child. However, few settings appreciate that they are accountable for the quality and reliability of the extended services they provide, and quality assurance of such provision remains under-developed.

Few local authorities evaluate thoroughly settings plans for developing extended services. Monitoring the impact of services provided in children's centres on the progress children make throughout their schooling is also limited in local authorities. School improvement advisers, in addition to the school improvement partners (SIPs), will need to have a focused discussion with school leaders about the evidence of the impact of extended service provision on pupils' learning and well-being.

One headteacher in the OFSTED HMI survey on extended services indicated that improvement was about creating a learning climate and community regeneration (OFSTED 2006c: 17).

Example of an extended school evaluation profile

Table 7.3 is an example of an extended school evaluation profile which is focused on the aims, collaborative culture and environment for partnership working.

Table 7.3 Example of an extended school evaluation profile for partnership working (Adapted from Coleman, A. 2006)

Aspect to be evaluated	**Developing** ✓	**Fully achieved** ✓
The extended school's aims are clearly expressed		
These aims are shared by all staff		
The aims have been developed in partnership		

Table 7.3 *(Continued)*

Aspect to be evaluated	**Developing** ✓	**Fully achieved** ✓
Aims are owned by partner staff		
Aims are clearly understood by key target groups		
Staff appreciate the demands of partner agencies		
Staff have a good understanding of partners' language and culture		
Staff understand the need for collaboration and are committed to it		
Colleagues from other organisations are valued		
The environmental needs of staff from other agencies working in school are understood		
Adequate resources are provided to enable colleagues to work effectively		
Environmental constraints to collaboration have been addressed		

(Source: Adapted from Coleman, A. NCSL, 2006, *Collaborative Leadership in Extended Schools. Leading in a multi-agency environment*, page 58)

Cameo of an extended school engaging with self-evaluation

ContinYou/DfES in their leaflet *Evidence and Evaluation* (2005e) gave an excellent example of a secondary school in Liverpool, which had developed good practice in data collection, monitoring and evaluating the impact of its out-of-school-hours study support programme.

Attendance figures collected monthly for study support activities indicated how many, and which pupils attended such activities by year group, gender and free school meals. The monthly data collected also recorded the number of hours pupils spent in each year group on every activity and the nature of the activities they were attending, e.g. academic, residential and/or leisure.

Using this data enabled the school to identify if there were any gender issues arising, and they found that girls were not attending the ICT club, so they set up an ICT club for girls and an ICT club for boys, in addition to the existing mixed-gender ICT after-school club.

The involvement of pupils in monitoring not only their own progress but in evolving their own clubs was also undertaken in the same school. Pupils in personal, social and health education (PSHE) set themselves personal targets and commented on the study support activities and clubs they had attended. This information was analysed to inform future study support provision.

Pupils could also contribute ideas and suggestions for new school clubs and activities by putting their suggestions on 'post-it' notes and placing these in the suggestion boxes around the school.

Pupils at the school were able to access their estimated grades via the school intranet. If a pupil found that they were not doing as well as they expected in a subject, they could click on the individual subject which then provided an online link to an updated diary of study support activities available for that particular subject, which the pupil could access for extra help.

The school had achieved an Advanced Level Award from the Quality in Study Support (QiSS) Recognition Scheme run by Canterbury Christ Church University, based on a process of self-evaluation against the framework of the Study Support Code of Practice. Further information and advice on how to develop study support programmes is available at: www.standards.dfes.gov.uk/studysupport and also at: www.continyou.org.uk/content.php?CategoryID=757

Further information about the QiSS scheme is available at:
www.canterbury.ac.uk/education/quality-in-study-support/

Each School participating in QiSS has to produce a portfolio of evidence that demonstrates that it meets the standards for each section of the Study Support Code of Practice at one of three levels: Emerging, Established and Advanced. A quality mark is gained at each level.

Canterbury Christ Church University has developed a quality assurance scheme for extended schools, based on similar lines to that of the QiSS process. This is known as the Quality in Extended Schools (QES) scheme. Schools participating in this scheme self-evaluate their extended school provision against the Extended School Code of Practice using the Quality Development Framework, which is aligned to the *Every Child Matters* five outcomes. Further information about QES can be found at:
www.canterbury.ac.uk/education/quality-in-study-support/extended-schools/

Participation in QiSS and QES would enable schools to gain external recognition and reward for developing their capacity to adapt to local circumstances, in providing quality extended service provision to meet the needs of the community.

The following monitoring and evaluation checklist provides a quick point of reference for school leaders and heads of children's centres.

Monitoring and evaluation checklist

- ❑ **You have built in monitoring and evaluation from the start.**
- ❑ **You have ensured everyone involved understands the monitoring, and evaluation process being utilised.**
- ❑ **There is a named person(s) responsible for monitoring and evaluating outcomes.**
- ❑ **There are robust procedures in place for systematically recording what is to be evaluated.**
- ❑ **Clear, agreed and shared objectives are used for monitoring and evaluating impact and outcomes.**
- ❑ **You are involving an external evaluator(s) in the process to present an objective view.**
- ❑ **You are monitoring and evaluating the effectiveness of partnership working in addition to service outcomes.**
- ❑ **All key stakeholders are involved in the evaluation process.**
- ❑ **There is an agreed and known timescale for reporting back outcomes.**
- ❑ **There are clear systems in place for feeding back the results from monitoring and evaluation throughout the year and at the end, which are in an accessible form.**
- ❑ **There are clear plans and procedures in place for celebrating achievements from the extended school/children's centre activities.**

Quality assurance through inspection aligned with National Standards and *Every Child Matters* outcomes

The requirement to evaluate and report on the school's or children's centre's contributions to the *Every Child Matters* outcomes and other related national standards of quality includes an evaluation of the extent to which extended services and wrap-around care contribute to children, young people's learning and well-being.

OFSTED will seek the views of service users, service providers, and in discussion with the school leadership team or head of children's centre will want to know:

- why the setting decided to offer the particular extended opportunities and additional service provision;
- how the extended school/children's centre service provision is impacting on standards and achievement;
- how the extended school activities and children's centre provision is improving the five *Every Child Matters* outcomes for children and young people;
- how well the extended school/children's centre activities and services are being used.

In particular, schools need to have sufficient evidence about the impact of the various initiatives relating to extended service provision to feed into the school's self-evaluation form (SEF). For example:

> If the homework club the school provides enables children to achieve higher standards, to enjoy the challenge of completing demanding work and to behave better in class, the SEF is the place to make that evaluation. If the school provides after-school classes in English as an additional language because there is nothing in the community to support Bangladeshi parents, the SEF is the place to show how you have evaluated the impact of this. What difference has such a venture made to children in the school?
>
> (OFSTED 2006a: 2)

Full day care: National Standards for under-8s day care and childminding

The 14 National Standards for under-8s day care and childminding, which includes full day care, sessional day care, crèches; out-of-school care and childminders, represent a baseline of quality below which no provider may fall.

Out-of-school care is defined as the facilities that provide day care for children under eight, which operate during one or more of the following periods: before school, after school, during the school holidays. The total care provided must be for more than two hours in any day and for more than five days per year.

OFSTED inspectors will have regard to these National Standards during Inspection, and will issue guidance on how the outcomes required by these standards may be achieved in settings where day care and childminding are provided.

The National Service Framework Standards for Children, Young People and Maternity Services

The National Service Framework (NSF) comprises of 11 quality standards for health, social care and some education services. They cover children and young people from birth to 19. Standards 1 to 5 are universal. Standards 6 to 10 cover services for children and young people requiring more specialised care, treatment and support. Standard 11 relates to pregnant women and their partners. The NSF aims to ensure high-quality and integrated health and social care from pregnancy through to adulthood. It promotes and supports a holistic child-centred approach to early identification, prevention and enabling children and young people to realise their full potential. The evidence-based NSF Standards feed into the school and children's centre self-evaluation process, in relation to indicating how the additional extended provision and services have impacted upon and improved the *Every Child Matters* five outcomes for children and young people.

The *Every Child Matters* outcomes

The five outcomes for children and young people have legal force through the Children Act 2004. They adopt a holistic child-centred approach to focus on the learning and well-being of children and young people. The five outcomes relate to: being healthy, staying safe, enjoying and achieving, making a positive contribution, and achieving economic well-being.

OFSTED in the inspection of LA children's services, schools, PRUs, children's centres, nurseries and other settings providing childcare, will focus on how far they meet the five *Every Child Matters* outcomes. This evidence will be obtained through direct observation, discussion with key stakeholders, as well as through the self-evaluation process, e.g. the SEF. The following parallels framework will enable schools and children's centres to evaluate their extended provision and services against the key National Standards. This will help schools and other settings to identify strengths in their provision, in addition to the areas and aspects requiring further improvement and development.

Table 7.4 Parallels evaluation framework for extended school services and children's centre provision (Adapted from and modelled on QES 2006)

Every Child Matters **Outcomes**	**National Service Framework Standards**	**National Standards for under 8s Day Care and Childminding**	**OFSTED SEF** (relevant aspects)
1. Be Healthy Children and young people ▪ physically healthy; ▪ sexually healthy; ▪ lead healthy lifestyles; ▪ choose not to take illegal drugs; ▪ parents, carers and families promote healthy choices.	**Standard 1 – Promoting health and well-being, identifying needs and intervening early** The health and well-being of all children and young people is promoted and delivered through a co-ordinated programme of action, including prevention and early intervention wherever possible, to ensure long-term gain, led by the NHS in partnership with LAs. **Standard 6 – Children and Young People Who are Ill** All children and young people who are ill, or thought to be ill or injured will have timely access to appropriate advice and effective services which address their health, social, educational and emotional needs throughout the period of their illness. **Standard 7 – Children and Young People in Hospital** Children and young people receive high-quality, evidence-based hospital care, developed through clinical governance and delivered in appropriate settings. **Standard 9 – The Mental Health and Psychological Well-being of Children and Young People** All children and young people, from birth to their eighteenth birthday, who have mental health problems and disorders have access to timely, integrated, high-quality, multi-disciplinary mental health services to ensure effective assessment, treatment and support, for them and their families.	**Standard 7 – Health** The registered person promotes the good health of children and takes positive steps to prevent the spread of infection and appropriate measures when they are ill. **Standard 8 – Food and Drink** Children are provided with regular drinks and food in adequate quantities for their needs. Food and drink is properly prepared, nutritious and complies with dietary and religious requirements.	**4a.** How well learners make progress in their personal development. **4b.** The extent to which learners adopt a healthy lifestyle, where appropriate. **4g.** On the basis of the self-evaluation, what are the key priorities for learners' personal development in relation to extended service provision.

Table 7.4 *(Continued)*

Every Child Matters **Outcomes**	**National Service Framework Standards**	**National Standards for under 8s Day Care and Childminding**	**OFSTED SEF** (relevant aspects)
1. **Be Healthy** (*continued*)	**Standard 10 – Medicines for Children and Young People** Children, young people, their parents or carers and health care professionals in all settings make decisions about medicines based on sound information about risk and benefit. They have access to safe and effective medicines that are prescribed on the basis of the best available evidence. **Standard 11 – Maternity Services** Women have easy access to supportive, high-quality maternity services, designed around their individual needs and those of their babies.		
2. **Stay Safe** Children and young people are: ▪ safe from maltreatment, neglect, violence and sexual exploitation; ▪ safe from accidental injury and death; ▪ safe from bullying and discrimination; ▪ safe from crime and anti-social behaviour in and out of school; ▪ have security, stability and are cared for; ▪ parents, carers and families provide safe homes and stability.	**Standard 5 – Safeguarding and Promoting the Welfare of Children and Young People** All agencies work to prevent children suffering harm and to promote their welfare, to provide them with the services they require to address their identified needs and safeguard children who are being, or are likely to be harmed.	**Standard 4 – Physical Environment** The premises are safe, secure and suitable for their purpose. They provide adequate space in an appropriate location, are welcoming to children and offer access to the necessary facilities for a range of activities, which promote their development. **Standard 5 – Equipment** Furniture, equipment and toys are provided which are appropriate for their purpose and help to create an accessible and stimulating environment. They are of suitable design and condition, well maintained and conform to safety standards.	**4c.** The extent to which learners feel safe and adopt safe practices.

Table 7.4 *(Continued)*

Every Child Matters **Outcomes**	**National Service Framework Standards**	**National Standards for under 8s Day Care and Childminding**	**OFSTED SEF** (relevant aspects)
2. Stay Safe (*continued*)		**Standard 6 – Safety** The registered person takes positive steps to promote safety within their setting and on outings, and ensures proper precautions are taken to prevent accidents. **Standard 13 – Child Protection** The registered person complies with local child protection procedures approved by the Area Child Protection Committee and ensures that all adults working and looking after children in the provision are able to put the procedures into practice.	
3. Enjoy and Achieve Children and young people: ■ are ready for school; ■ attend and enjoy school; ■ achieve stretching national educational standards at primary school; ■ achieve personal and social development and enjoy recreation; ■ achieve stretching national educational standards at secondary school; ■ have parents, carers and families support learning.		**Standard 3 – Care, Learning and Play** The registered person meets children's individual needs and promotes their welfare. They plan and provide activities and play opportunities to develop children's emotional, physical, social and intellectual capabilities.	**3a.** What learners' achievements and standards are in extended service provision. **3c.** On the basis of the evaluation, the key priorities for extended service development. **5a.** How good the quality of teaching and learning is in extended school provision. **5b.** How well extended service provision meets the range of needs and interests of learners and users.

Table 7.4 *(Continued)*

Every Child Matters **Outcomes**	**National Service Framework Standards**	**National Standards for under 8s Day Care and Childminding**	**OFSTED SEF** (relevant aspects)
4. Make a Positive Contribution Children and young people: ▪ engage in decision making and support the community and environment; ▪ engage in law-abiding and positive behaviour in and out of school; ▪ develop positive relationships and choose not to bully or discriminate; ▪ develop self-confidence and successfully deal with significant life changes and challenges; ▪ develop enterprising behaviour; ▪ parents, carers and families promote positive behaviour.	**Standard 8 – Disabled Children and Young People and Those with Complex Health Needs** Children and young people who are disabled or who have complex health needs receive co-ordinated, high-quality child and family-centred services which are based on assessed needs, promote social inclusion and, where possible, enable them and their families to live ordinary lives. **Standard 2 – Supporting Parenting** Parents or carers are enabled to receive the information, services and support which will help them to care for their children and equip them with the skills they need to ensure that their children have optimum life chances and are healthy and safe.	**Standard 9 – Equal opportunities** The registered person and staff actively provide equality of opportunity and anti-discriminatory practice for all children. **Standard 10 – Special needs (including SEN and disabilities)** The registered person is aware that some children may have special needs and is proactive in ensuring that appropriate action can be taken when such a child is identified or admitted to the provision. Steps are taken to promote the welfare and development of the child within the setting in partnership with the parents and other relevant parties. **Standard 11 – Behaviour** Adults caring for children in the provision are able to manage a wide range of children's behaviour in a way which promotes their welfare and development. **Standard 12 – Working in Partnership with Parents and Carers** The registered person and staff work in partnership with parents to meet the needs of the children, both individually and as a group. Information is shared.	**2a.** How the views of learners, parents/carers and other stakeholders are gathered. **2b.** What the views gathered tell you about the standards and quality of the extended activities and services provided. **2c.** How the collected findings about extended service provision are shared with parents/carers and other stakeholders. **2d.** Examples of action taken based on the views of learners, parents/carers and other stakeholders, with an evaluation of the effectiveness of what you did. **4d.** How well learners make a positive contribution to the community.

Table 7.4 *(Continued)*

***Every Child Matters* Outcomes**	**National Service Framework Standards**	**National Standards for under 8s Day Care and Childminding**	**OFSTED SEF** (relevant aspects)
5. Achieve Economic Well-being Children and young people: ■ engage in further education, employment or training on leaving school; ■ are ready for employment; ■ live in decent homes and sustainable communities; ■ have access to transport and material goods; ■ live in households free from low income; ■ have parents, carers and families who are supported to be economically active.	**Standard 4 – Growing Up into Adulthood** All young people have access to age-appropriate services, which are responsive to their specific needs as they grow into adulthood.		**4e.** How well learners prepare for their future economic well-being. **5c.** How well learners are guided and supported.
Other aspects – (context, leadership and management, organisation and documentation)	**Standard 3 – Child, Young Person and Family-centred Services** Children and young people and families receive high-quality services, which are co-ordinated around their individual and family needs and take account of their views.	**Standard 1 – Suitable person** Adults providing day care looking after children or having unsupervised access to them are suitable to do so. **Standard 2 – Organisation** The registered person meets required adult to child ratios, ensures that training and qualifications requirements are met and organises space and resources to meet the children's needs effectively. **Standard 14 – Documentation** Records, policies and procedures, which are required for the efficient	**1b.** Aims, range of extended services. **1c.** Contextual issues creating barriers or acting as aids to extended school services, e.g. recruitment and retention of staff, procuring third-party providers, amalgamation or co-location. **1d.** Additional characteristics related to extended service provision, e.g. local reputation of extended service provision. **1e.** Main priorities for extended service provision. **5d.** The quality of extended service and day-care provision.

Table 7.4 *(Continued)*

***Every Child Matters* Outcomes**	**National Service Framework Standards**	**National Standards for under 8s Day Care and Childminding**	**OFSTED SEF** (relevant aspects)
		and safe management of the provision, or to promote the welfare, care and learning of children, are maintained. Records about individual children are shared with the child's parent(s).	**5e.** On the basis of self-evaluation, the key priorities for improving the quality of extended service provision. **6a.** Overall effectiveness and efficiency of leadership and management of extended service provision. **6c.** On the basis of self-evaluation, the key priorities for leadership and management of extended service provision. **7a.** Overall effectiveness of extended service provision with its main strengths and weaknesses. **7b.** Steps taken to promote improvement in extended service provision since the previous inspection. **7c.** Capacity available to meet further improvement in extended service provision. **7d.** Steps required to further improve extended service provision.

Collecting qualitative evidence from service users and providers – model surveys

EXTENDED SCHOOL PROVISION PUPIL SURVEY

Extended school activities and services take place before and after school, at lunchtimes, at weekends and during school holidays.

Please answer the following questions
(√ the relevant boxes)

I am Male ☐ I am Female ☐ My age is ☐

1. I attend the following out of school hours clubs and activities

   Breakfast Club ☐ Study Support ☐ Homework Club ☐ Sports Activities ☐ Music Clubs ☐ Easter School ☐

   Health & Fitness Club ☐ Youth Club ☐ Special Interest clubs ☐ Cultural Visits ☐ Summer School ☐

   Other ☐ Please specify ____________________

   ____

2. The out of school activity I have enjoyed the **most** has been ____________________

3. The out of school activity I have **least** enjoyed is ____________________

   because: ____________________

4. I think there is a good range of out of school hours activities on offer

   YES☐ NO ☐

5. I would like to see the school offering the following extended activities:

   ____

   ____

6. I would be interested in attending more activities at the weekend or in school holidays

   YES☐ NO ☐

7. I would be interested in doing after school activities together with my parents/family

   YES☐ NO ☐

8. I would like my parents/carers to become more involved in helping me with my learning

   YES☐ NO ☐

9. Is there anything else you wish to comment on about out-of-school-hours activities?

   ____

   ____

Thanks for your time in answering these questions

Please give your completed survey to the Extended School Coordinator

Figure 7.2 Extended school provision pupil survey

EXTENDED SCHOOL PROVISION SERVICE USER SURVEY

Please answer the following questions
Place a √ in the relevant boxes

I am Male ☐ I am Female ☐ My age is ☐ My postcode is ☐

1. I have attended the following activities and services at the school
   Adult Learning ☐ Parent Workshops ☐ ICT Club ☐ Sports Activities ☐ Music Arts activities ☐ Parent Information Centre ☐

   Creche ☐ Nursery Childcare ☐ Cyber Café ☐ Special Interest clubs ☐

   Other ☐ Please specify ______

2. The activity/service I have enjoyed the **most** ______
3. The activity/service I have **least** enjoyed ______

   because: ______
4. I would like to see the school offering the following new activities/services for adults

   ______

   ______
5. Access to activities and services could be improved by:

   ______

   ______
6. I would be interested in joining a parents/community group to help plan extended services
   YES ☐ NO ☐
7. I know who to contact at the school if I have any queries about extended services
   YES ☐ NO ☐
8. The basic amenities, i.e. toilets, and facilities for refreshments are of a good standard
   YES ☐ NO ☐
9. Communication, information & publicity material about extended school provision is helpful
   YES ☐ NO ☐
10. The charges made for extended school activities and services offer good value for money
    YES ☐ NO ☐

11 I would be willing to help run and deliver a school club
   YES ☐ NO ☐

12. Is there anything else you wish to comment on about extended school provision?

    ______

    ______

Thank you for completing this survey

Please return your survey to the main school office

Figure 7.3 Extended school provision service user survey

EXTENDED SCHOOL PROVISION SERVICE PROVIDER SURVEY

Please answer the following questions.

1. How does the extended service or activity you provide meet the clients with the greatest needs?

2. How has the activity or service met the extended school programme goals?

3. What has been the impact of the service/activity you have delivered on clients?

4. How well has the service or activity been received by the clients/users?

5. How has the activity or service provided by you met the Every Child Matters outcomes?

6. How is the service or activity contributing to early intervention and prevention?

7. If the service/activity is chargeable, does it offer good value for money, and should the charging fee be increased?

8. Have there been any barriers to the implementation and delivery of the service or activity you have offered to clients?

9. If there were barriers in implementation, how could these be overcome/resolved?

10. Are there any activities or aspects of extended provision that you have offered, which you consider should not be included in next years programme?

11. Any further comments or suggestions relating to extended school provision?

Thank you for taking the time to complete this survey

Please return your survey to the Extended School Coordinator

Figure 7.4 Extended school provision service provider survey

Further activities for school leaders and heads of children's centres

The following questions are designed to enable you to discuss and identify the extended services and activities that have been most effective in meeting the needs of children, young people, families and the community, and those that require further development in order to improve future service provision.

- Which have been the most successful extended activities and services and why?
- What areas or aspects of extended school or children's centre provision require improvement and how will you address this?
- Which extended school activities or children's centre services have been poorly attended and how do you intend to resolve this issue?
- What have been the greatest gains and outcomes for children, young people, families and the community in relation to the extended school/children's centre activities and services provided?
- What have been the main barriers to clients accessing services and activities, and how do you intend to improve this aspect?
- What problems, if any, have arisen in relation to services and activities being provided and delivered by other partners and agencies, and how do you intend to resolve the difficulties that may have arisen?
- What trends or priorities have you identified that need addressing in the future extended school/children's centre service provision within your setting?
- How is the evidence of impact of extended school and children's centre provision disseminated and used as part of the process of review and development?
- How could your quality assurance process be further improved in order to demonstrate best value and the value-added progress gained from extended school and children's centre provision delivered in your setting?
- What lessons have your learned about the provision of quality extended school and children's centre services?
- How do you really know that your extended school services and/or children's centre provision is making a real difference to children, young people and their families?
- What key outcomes for extended school/children's centre provision have you achieved?
- What impact have your extended school activities and/or children's centre provision had in meeting the needs of children, young people, staff and the community? How do you know?
- What kind of reputation does the extended school activities/children's centre service provision have in the community and how do you know?
- How good is the delivery of your extended school/children's centre provision?
- How good is the management of extended school/children's centre provision?
- How good is the leadership of extended school activities and children's centre service provision?
- What is your capacity for further improvement in relation to extended school/children's centre provision?

Glossary

Additional needs – describes all children at risk of poor outcomes in relation to the *Every Child Matters* five outcomes for children and young people, and who require extra support from education, health or social services for a limited time or on a longer-term basis.

Agency – a statutory or voluntary organisation where staff, who are paid or unpaid, work with or have access to children, young people and families.

At risk – describes a child believed and thought to be at risk of significant harm, social exclusion or offending, who requires protection from the local authority and other services/agencies.

Brokerage – describes the act of arranging or negotiating relationships and partnerships within and beyond a network. A broker is an intermediary. Local authorities often take on this role, as well as Sure Start, diocesan boards, and Excellence in Cities.

Children's centre – a one-stop shop and community service hub for parents/carers and children under five, offering early education and childcare, family support, health services, employment advice and specialist support on a single site to improve their life chances.

Children's trusts – help to bring together schools with specialist support services, voluntary and community sector providers, who can help, and they broker imaginative solutions to provision.

Collaboration – is a process of working jointly with others, including those with whom one is not normally or immediately connected, to develop and achieve common goals.

Commissioning – is the process of assessing needs, allocating resources, defining priorities and choices and determining how they are best delivered, monitoring implementation and delivery, evaluating impact and learning from the process.

DEMOS – is an independent think-tank which connects researchers, thinkers and practitioners to an international network of people changing politics. It works with any organisation that can make change happen from schools to companies and the government.

Disabled – any individual who has a physical or mental impairment, which has a substantial and long-term adverse effect on his/her ability to carry out normal day-to-day activities.

Education Improvement Partnership – gives unity and a sharper purpose to collaboration across schools to tackle common issues such as: 14–19 provision, behaviour improvement, childcare and extended services. Between five to thirty schools can be in an EIP.

Engagement – involving the customer/user (children, young people and families) in the design and delivery of services and decisions that affect them.

Evaluation – is concerned with gauging effectiveness, strengths and weaknesses, and interpreting how well things are going.

Extended school – offers a range of core universal services and out-of-hours activities to meet the needs of children, young people, families and the wider community.

Family learning – provides courses specifically designed for parents or other carers to attend with their children.

Federation – refers to a group of two or more schools with a formal agreement to work together to raise standards.

Focus group – comprises of six to eight participants who represent a cross-section of the school's/children's centre community. Their purpose is to listen to views of group members and to obtain information on particular topics.

Inclusion – concerns the quality of children's experience, how they are helped to learn, achieve and participate fully in the life of the school/setting, and within the community, irrespective of where they are educated.

Information sharing – passing on relevant information to other agencies, organisations and individuals that require it in order to deliver better services to children and young people.

Key worker – refers to a practitioner from health, social care or education services who provides a lead support and advocacy role to children and young people with more complex needs.

Lead professional – a designated professional (from health, social care or education services), who has day-to-day contact with a child/young person, and who co-ordinates and monitors service provision, acting as a gatekeeper for information sharing.

Local Area Agreements – set out the priorities for a local area agreed between central government and a local area (the local authority and Local Strategic Partnership) and other key partners at the local level. They help to join up public services more effectively.

Local Strategic Partnerships – are a core component of the national Neighbourhood Renewal Strategy. They are cross-sectoral, cross-agency, umbrella partnerships that bring together the private, public, voluntary and community sectors to provide a single overarching local co-ordination framework within which other, more specific local partnerships can operate.

Monitoring – checking progress against targets, looking out for trends in performance indicators and seeing that strategies have been implemented.

Multi-agency working – is where those from more than one agency or service work together jointly, sharing aims, information, tasks and responsibilities.

Networking – is a process that helps to promote innovation and change through collaboration, sharing best practice, expertise and resources.

One-stop-shop – is capable of supplying all a customer's needs within a particular range of goods or services in one place.

Outcomes – refers to the identifiable (positive or negative) impact of interventions, programmes or services on children and young people. It also refers to the five *Every Child Matters* outcomes.

Personalisation – is where users are active participants in the shaping, development and delivery of education and related services. It creates more involved and responsible users.

Remodelling – is a structured change process which empowers teams to tackle their key opportunities and issues in a way that reflects their local circumstances.

Social capital – refers to the norms of trust, the connections among individuals and the networks of reciprocal social relations that enable collective action.

Specialist services – include child protection services, adoption and fostering services for looked after children and their families, residential services and services for children with serious mental health problems such as eating disorders. These services are provided specifically for children with acute or high level needs who would otherwise be at a high risk of achieving poor outcomes.

Stakeholder – any person, group, organisation or institution that has an interest in an activity, project or programme. This includes intended beneficiaries and intermediaries, winners and losers and those involved or excluded from the decision making process.

Study support – describes the very wide range of activities and opportunities offered by schools around their 'normal' day, which may take place at school or elsewhere, enhancing and enriching children's experience and contributing to their higher attainment.

Sure Start – established in 1999, refers to the extensive government programme to eradicate child poverty in the most deprived areas, with the aim of improving the health and well-being of families and children from birth to five, in Children's Centres.

Sustainability – is the capacity of a system to engage in the complexities of continuous improvement consistent with deep values of human purpose. It is also the continuation in the benefits produced by a project or initiative after it has ended.

Systems leadership – takes an outward-facing and system-oriented perspective, which has a moral purpose, and a commitment to building lateral capacity through collaboration and networking.

Targeted services – provide support for children less likely to achieve optimal outcomes who have additional needs, or complex needs, ideally within universal settings such as Children's Centres and Full-Service Extended Schools.

Universal services – also known as mainstream services, are provided and made routinely available to all children, young people and their families, which includes Early Years provision, mainstream schools and Connexions, GPs, midwives and health visitors.

Value-added progress – looks at rates of progress over time in addition to attainment, in relation to prior attainment or starting points.

Vulnerable children – refers to those children and young people at risk of social exclusion, those who are disadvantaged and whose life chances are likely to be jeopardised unless action is taken to meet their needs better. This includes those in public care, children with learning difficulties and disabilities, travellers, asylum seekers, excluded pupils, truants, young offenders, young family carers, children living in families experiencing stress, children affected by domestic violence.

Wrap-around care/childcare – this refers to provision that is 'wrapped around' the normal school day (or the free entitlement to integrated early learning and care for three and four-year-olds), which is offered through schools, children's centres, nurseries, registered childminders or approved childcarers.

Useful Websites and Resources

www.basic-skills.co.uk

www.chartermark.gov.uk

www.childpolicy.org.uk

www.communitycare.co.uk

www.continyou.org.uk/esdocs

www.continyou.org.uk/oshlresources

www.dfes.gov.uk/studysupport/

www.everychildmatters.gov.uk

www.4children.org.uk

www.inclusion.org.uk

www.inclusionmark.co.uk

www.ncsl.org.uk

www.neighbourhood.statistics.gov.uk

www.ofsted.gov.uk/publications

www.qiss.org.uk

www.surestart.gov.uk

www.teachernet.gov.uk/extendedschools

www.teachers.tv/home.do

www.tloltd.co.uk

Teachers TV website has three 15-minute programme videos to watch online or download, related to extended schools:

- Primary Extended Schools – Whole-Community Outreach
- School Matters – Extended Schools
- Primary Extended Schools – Opening Doors

The NCSL Challenge Workshops 2006–07 related to leading extended schools, focusing on community collaboration, multi-agency working and parent and children power, will publish their outcomes on the NCSL website.

References and Further Reading

ASCL (2006) Press release on extended schooling – ASCL/Governors' Association Conference June 14. Association of School and College Lecturers.

ATL (2004) *Extended Schools. Position Statement.* London: Association of Teachers and Lecturers.

Barber, M. and Fullan, M. (2005) *Tri-Level Development. It's the System.* London: Education Week.

Brindle, D. (2006) 'Extended or Stretched?', *The Guardian*, May 16, p. 13.

Brindle, D. (2006) 'Growing Pains and Changing Roles', *The Guardian*, Society Guardian, May 17, p. 1.

Brown, K. and White, K. (2006) *Exploring the Evidence Base for Integrated Children's Services.* Edinburgh: Scottish Executive Education Department.

Calfee, C., Wittwer, F. and Meredith, M. (1998) *Building A Full-Service School: A Step-by-Step Guide.* San Fransisco: Jossey-Bass.

Cambridge Education (2006) *Making Every Child Matter Resource Pack*, Section 2 The Audit. Cambridge: Cambridge Education Limited.

Campbell, C. and Whitty, G. (2002) 'Inter-Agency Collaborations for Inclusive Schooling', pp. 109–10, in *Developing Inclusive Schooling. Perspectives, Policies and Practices.* London: Institute of Education, University of London.

Carter, K., Franey, T. and Payne, G. (2006) *Reshaping the Landscape. Exploring the Challenges of Outward-Facing Leadership with a System Perspective*, in NEXUS pp. 34–6. Nottingham: National College for School Leadership.

Coles, C. and Hancock, R. (2002) *The Inclusion Quality Mark.* Bristol: TLO Limited.

Coleman, A. (2006) *Collaborative Leadership in Extended Schools. Leading in a Multi-Agency Environment.* Nottingham: National College for School Leadership.

Collarbone, P. (2005) Speech at the Target 2010 Conference – 'Extended Schools and Sure Start Children's Centres'. London: National Remodelling Team.

Constable, D. (2002) *Planning and Organising the SENCO Year.* London: David Fulton Publishers.

ContinYou (2003) *Top Tips. Bright Ideas for Involving People from the Local Community in your Out-Of-School-Hours Clubs.* London: ContinYou.

ContinYou (2004) *Family Learning in Primary Schools*, PowerPoint presentation by Firs Hill Community Primary School, slides 2 and 7. London: ContinYou.

ContinYou (2005a) *Fundraising Guidance. Study Support/Out-Of-School-Hours Learning (oshl).* Coventry: ContinYou.

ContinYou (2005b) *The Support Service for Schools. Consultation.* London: The Extended School Support Service (TESSS)/ContinYou.

ContinYou (2006) '*Extended Services. Putting the Pieces Together*', pp. 9–11, in *Schools etc Extending to Communities*, Issue 1. London: ContinYou.

ContinYou/DfES (2004) *Accounting for VAT.* London: Department for Education and Skills.

ContinYou/DfES (2005a) *Governors' Roles and Governance.* London: ContinYou/Department for Education and Skills.

ContinYou/DfES (2005b) *Use of School Premises by Third Party Providers.* London: ContinYou/Department for Education and Skills.

ContinYou/DfES (2005c) *Involving and Working with Voluntary and Community-Sector Organisations.* London: ContinYou/Department for Education and Skills.

ContinYou/DfES (2005d) *Welcoming the Whole Community.* London: ContinYou/Department for Education and Skills.

ContinYou/DfES (2005e) *Evidence and Evaluation.* London: ContinYou/Department for Education and Skills.

ContinYou/DfES (2005f) *School Companies.* London: ContinYou/Department for Education and Skills.

ContinYou/DfES (2005g) *Extending the School's ICT to the Community.* London: ContinYou/Department for Education and Skills.

ContinYou/DfES (2005h) *Consultation.* London: ContinYou/Department for Education and Skills.

ContinYou/DfES (2006) *Parenting Support.* London: ContinYou/Department for Education and Skills.

Craig, J., Huber, J. and Lownsbrough, H. (2004) *Schools Out. Can Teachers, Social Workers and Health Staff Learn to Live Together?* London: DEMOS.

Dabnor, J. and Robson, J. (2006) *QES: Quality Development Framework Criterion Parallels Document.* Canterbury: Canterbury Christ Church University.

Dearden, P.N. (2005) *An Introduction to Multi-Agency Planning Using the Logical Framework Approach.* Wolverhampton: Centre for International Development and Training (CIDT), University of Wolverhampton.

DfES (2001a) *The Impact of Study Support: A Study into the Effects of Participation in Out-Of-School-Hours Learning on the Academic Attainment, Attitudes and Attendance of Secondary School Students.* RB273. London: Department for Education and Skills.

DfES (2001b) *Health and Safety: Responsibilities and Powers.* London: Department for Education and Skills.

DfES (2001c) *Assessing the Net Capacity of Schools.* London: Department for Education and Skills.

DfES (2002a) *An Introduction. Extended Schools providing Opportunities and Services for All.* London: Department for Education and Skills.

DfES (2002b) *Extended Schools Providing Opportunities and Services for All.* London: Department for Education and Skills.

DfES (2002c) *A Study of Extended Schools Demonstration Projects.* RB381. London: Department for Education and Skills.

DfES (2003a) *Towards the Development of Extended Schools.* RB408. London: Department for Education and Skills.

DfES (2003b) *Towards Extended Schools: A Literature Review.* RR432. London: Department for Education and Skills.

DfES (2003c) *Extended Schools. The Role of the Childcare Coordinator.* RB457. London: Department for Education and Skills.

DfES (2003d) *School Complaints Procedure.* London: Department for Education and Skills.

DfES (2003e) *Extended Schools Pathfinder Evaluation: Issues for Schools and Local Education Authorities.* RBX18–03. London: Department for Education and Skills.

DfES (2003f) *Excellence and Enjoyment: A Strategy for Primary Schools.* London: Department for Education and Skills.

DfES (2003g) *Full Day Care: National Standards for under 8s Day Care and Childminding.* London: Department for Education and Skills.

DfES (2004a) *Lessons from Study Support for Compulsory Learning.* RB529. London: Department for Education and Skills.

DfES (2004b) *Evaluation of the Extended Schools Pathfinder Projects.* RB530. London: Department for Education and Skills.

DfES (2004c) *Five Year Strategy for Children and Learners.* London: Department for Education and Skills.

DfES (2004d) *Every Child Matters: Next Steps.* London: Department for Education and Skills.

DfES (2004e) *National Standards for Headteachers.* London: Department for Education and Skills.

DfES (2005a) *Education Improvement Partnerships: Local Collaboration for School Improvement and Better Service Delivery.* RB680. London: Department for Education and Skills.

DfES (2005b) *Realising Children's Trust Arrangements. National Evaluation of Children's Trusts Phase 1.* RR682. London: Department for Education and Skills.

DfES (2005c) *Early Impacts of Sure Start Local Programmes on Children and Families.* London: Department for Education and Skills.

DfES (2005d) *Variation in Sure Start Local Programmes' Effectiveness: Early Preliminary Findings.* London: Department for Education and Skills.

DfES (2005e) *Fact Sheet. Multi-Agency Working.* London: Department for Education and Skills.

DfES (2005f) *Extended Services in Schools: Baseline Survey of Maintained Schools in 2005.* London: Department for Education and Skills.

DfES (2005g) *Evaluation of the Full Service Extended Schools Pathfinder Project: End of First Year Report.* London: Department for Education and Skills.

DfES (2005h) *Extended Schools: Access to Opportunities and Services for All – A Prospectus.* London: Department for Education and Skills.

DfES (2005i) *Education Improvement Partnerships: Local Collaboration for School Improvement and Better Service Delivery.* London: Department for Education and Skills.

DfES (2005j) *A New Relationship with Schools: School Improvement Partners' Brief.* London: Department for Education and Skills.

DfES (2005k) *Guidance on School Companies.* London: Department for Education and Skills.

DfES (2005l) *Higher Standards, Better Schools for All.* London: Department for Education and Skills.

DfES (2005m) *Youth Matters Green Paper.* London: Department for Education and Skills.

DfES (2005n) *Youth Matters: Next Steps.* London: Department for Education and Skills.

DfES (2006a) *Safer School Partnerships – Mainstreaming.* London: Department for Education and Skills.

DfES (2006b) *Planning and Funding Extended Schools: A Guide for Schools, Local Authorities and their Partner Organisations.* London: Department for Education and Skills.

DfES (2006c) *Evaluation of the Full Service Extended Schools Initiative, Second Year: Thematic Papers.* London: Department for Education and Skills.

DfES/CA/ISBA (2005k) *Commercial Activities in Schools. Best Practice Principles.* London: Department for Education and Skills/Consumer Association/Incorporated Society of British Advertisers.

DfES/NCSL (2004d) *Systems Thinkers in Action: Moving beyond the Standards Plateau.* London: Department for Education and Skills Innovation Unit.

DfES/Sure Start (2005) *Research to Inform the Management and Governance of Children's Centres.* London: SQW Limited Department for Education and Skills.

Finch, S. (2006) 'Work life balance. Does it make a difference?', Slide 3 PowerPoint presentation at Creating Opportunities, Building Futures Conference, Consultancy 4 Children, March.

Frean, A. (2006) 'Parents Told to Pay for After-Hours School Clubs', *The Times,* June 7.

Fullan, M. (2002) 'The change leader', *Educational Leadership,* May 2002, EBSCO Publishing.

Fullan, M. (2004) 'Leadership Across the System', *Insight,* Winter 2004, pp. 14–17.

Fullan, M. (2005) 'Professional Learning Communities Writ Large', in *On Common Ground.* Bloomington, Indiana: National Education Service, pp. 209–32.

Guardian/Ed Coms (2006) ' "Headspace" headteachers' survey', April 2006. London: IMC Research.

Haywood, B., Chambers, M., Powell, G. and Baxter, G. (2006) *Ensuring Every Child Matters. Diagnostic and Planning Tools.* Bristol: TLO Limited.

HM Treasury (2004) *Choice for Parents, the Best Start for Children: A Ten Year Strategy for Childcare.* London: Her Majesty's Treasury, Crown Copyright.

Holman, R. (2004) 'Undo the Wrapping', *Community Care,* 21 October 2004, p. 1, www.communitycare.co.uk/Articles, accessed 30 July 2006.

IDeA (2004) *Show Me How I Matter,* Part 2, p. 17. London: Improvement and Development Agency.

IDeA (2006) Newsletter. *2. Planning for Excellence in Children's Services,* p. 2, June 2006. London: Improvement and Development Agency.

Kirham, S. (2006) Press release prior to ASCL/Governors' Association Conference on extended schooling, 14 June.

Last, G. (2004) *Personalising Learning: Adding Value to the Learning Journey through the Primary School.* London: Department for Education and Skills.

Leney, F. (2006) 'Heads Stretch to Open All Hours', p. 27. *Times Educational Supplement,* June 16.

Lindley, K. (2006) 'Community Conversation. Developing Extended Schools through Stakeholder Consultation', Research Associate Summary Report, Spring 2006. Nottingham: National College for School Leadership.

Ludvigsen, A. (2006) *More School, Less Play? The Role of Play in the Extended School in Denmark and England.* London: Barnardo's.

NAHT (2006a) *Extended Schools Extended Horizons. A Guidance Document from the National Association of Headteachers.* West Sussex: National Association of Headteachers.

NAHT (2006b) Briefing Paper 1. *Extended Schools.* NAHT Annual Conference 2006.

NCSL (2004) *Networked Leadership. Practice is the Heart of the Matter: Distributed Leadership and Networked Learning Communities.* Nottingham: National College for School Leadership.

NCSL (2005a) *Success and Sustainability: Developing the Strategically-Focused School.* Nottingham: National College for School Leadership.

NCSL (2005b) *Taking the Wide View. The New Leadership of Extended Schools.* Nottingham: National College for School Leadership.

NCSL (2005c) 'Shaping the Future: Remodelling Education to Meet Every Child's Needs', *Nexus,* Issue 5, p. 15. Nottingham: National College for School Leadership.

NCSL (2006a) *ECM. Why it Matters to Leaders.* Nottingham: National College for School Leadership.

NCSL (2006b) *Lessons from Extended Schools.* Nottingham: National College for School Leadership.

NCSL (2006c) 'School Leaders Leading the System', *NEXUS,* Special edition. Nottingham: National College for School Leadership.

NCSL (2006d) *National Standards for Leaders of Children's Centres,* Draft for Consultation. Bedfordshire: National College for School Leadership.

NCSL (2006e) *Community Conversation: Developing Extended Schools through Stakeholder Consultation,* Research Associate Summary Report, Spring 2006. Nottingham: National College for School Leadership.

NPHA (2005) *Every Child Matters,* Newsletter November/December 2005, London: National Primary Headteachers Association.

NRT (2005) *Extended Schools Remodelling Programme – An Introduction.* Extended Schools Launch Pack. London: National Remodelling Team.

NRT (2006) *Extended Schools – A Guide for Governors 1.* London: National Governors Association, National Remodelling Team.

OFSTED (2005) *Extended Schools: A Report on Early Developments.* HMI 2453. London: Office for Standards in Education.

OFSTED (2006a) *Maximising Impact: Developing Study Support/Out-Of-School-Hours Learning in a Fast-changing Learning Environment.* Chief HMI presentation, East Midlands Conference, University of Nottingham, March 29–30. London: Office for Standards in Education.

OFSTED (2006b) *Improving Performance through School Self-Evaluation and Improvement Planning. Further Guidance.* HMI 2466. London: Office for Standards in Education.

OFSTED (2006c) *Extended Services in Schools and Children's Centres.* HMI 2609. London: Office for Standards in Education.

Piper, J. (2005) *From Cutty Sark to Airbus – The Potential for Extended Schools and their Communities.* PowerPoint presentation. London: The Extended Schools Support Service/ ContinYou.

QES (2006) Quality Development Framework Criteria Parallels Document, Canterbury Christ Church University, February.

Research Foundation 4Children (2005) *Extended Schools Survey,* February 2005. London: 4Children.

Revell, P. (2006) 'Double Trouble for the Chiefs', p. 29. *Times Educational Supplement,* June 30.

Semmens, R.A. (1999) 'Full Service Schooling', Paper presented at the British Educational Research Association Conference, September 2–5, Brighton: University of Sussex.

SFYS (2002) *Making It Easy. Enhancing Partnerships through Protocols. A Guide for Developing Protocols between Schools and Services Based in the Community. Working Document.* Victoria: Department of Education and Training.

SHA (2004) Policy Paper 14, *Every Child Matters. Achieving Coherence and Consensus.* Leicester: Secondary Headteachers Association.

Shepherd, A. (2006) 'Under the Same Blanket', June 2, p. 29. *Times Educational Supplement.*

Society Guardian (2006) 'Growing Pains and Changing Role', 17 May, p. 2.

Stroud, V. (2004) *Extended Schools Remodelling Programme.* London: National Remodelling Team.

Sure Start (2005a) *Sure Start Children's Centres: Practice Guidance.* London: Sure Start.

Sure Start (2005b) *National Evaluation Summary. Implementing Sure Start Local Programmes: An Integrated Overview of the First Four Years.* London: Sure Start.

Sure Start (2006) *Children's Centres. Leading the Way,* Newsletter, Autumn 2006, p. 13.

Sylva, K., Melhuish, E. C., Sammons, P., Siraj-Blatchford, I., Taggart, B. (2004) *The Effective Provision of Pre-School Education (EPPE) Project: Technical Paper 12–The Final Report: Effective Pre-School Education.* London: Department for Education and Skills/Institute of Education, University of London.

TDA (2006a) *Extended Schools – What Does It Mean for Me?* London: Training and Development Agency for Schools.

TDA (2006b) *Extended Schools – Know-How.* London: Training and Development Agency for Schools.

Thompson, P. (2006) *Extended Schools, 'Extended Horizons'. A Guidance Document from NAHT,* 1 February, Presidential Seminar.

Tickle, L. (2006) 'Teacher Goes to Nursery', *The Guardian,* June 6, p. 13.

Times Educational Supplement (2006) 'Nursery School with Knobs on', 21 April, p. 27.

WAMG (2005) *Note 11: Every Child Matters and Extended Schools.* London: Workforce Agreement Monitoring Group.

Waterman, C. (2004) *Ten: Every School Matters.* London: The Education Network.

West-Burnham, J. and Coates, M. (2005) *Personalising Learning. Transforming Education for Every Child.* Stafford: Network Educational Press.

Whalley, M. (2005) *Developing Leadership Approaches for Early Years Settings*, PowerPoint presentation – Leading Together, April 2005. National College for School Leadership.

Whalley, M. (2006) *Children's Centres: The New Frontier for the Welfare State and the Education System? Engaging with the Struggle.* Early Interventions for Infants and Small Children in Families at Risk Conference. Norway: National College for School Leadership.

Whittaker, M. (2006) 'Nursery School with Knobs On', *Times Educational Supplement*, April 21.

Index